Marginal Sights

Marginal

Staging the Chinese in America

Studies in Theatre History and Culture

Edited by Thomas Postlewait

Sights

James S. Moy

University of Iowa Press ⨈ Iowa City

University of Iowa Press, Iowa City 52242
Printed in the United States of America

Design by Richard Hendel
Printed on acid-free paper

Library of Congress Cataloging-in-Publication Data

Moy, James S.

Marginal sights: staging the Chinese in America / by
James S. Moy.

   p.   cm. — (Studies in theatre history and culture)
Includes bibliographical references.
ISBN 0-87745-427-2, ISBN 0-87745-448-5 paper

1. American literature — Chinese influences.
2. United States — Civilization — Chinese
influences.   3. American literature — History
and criticism.   4. Chinese Americans in literature.
5. Theater — United States — History.   6. Chinese
in literature.   7. China in literature.   I. Title.
II. Series.
PS159.C5M69   1993
973'.004951 — dc20   93-17415
97 96 95 94 93   C   5   4   3   2   1
97 96   P   5   4   3   2

For Jennifer,

My darling little baby girl.

May the future be so bright

You'll need sunglasses.

Contents

Acknowledgments

Sections from chapters and early versions of several parts of this project have appeared as journal articles. Portions of "The Panoptic Empire of the Gaze: Authenticity and the Touristic Siting of Chinese America" recently appeared in *Modern Drama* 35 (1992) under the title "The Anthropological Gaze and the Touristic Siting of Chinese America." A version of "Bret Harte and Mark Twain's *Ah Sin*: Locating China in the Geography of the American West" appeared under the same title in *Studies in Chinese-Western Comparative Drama*, ed. Yun-Tong Luk (Hong Kong: Chinese University Press, 1990). "*Casualties of War*: The Death of Asia on the American Field of Representation" came out under a similar title in *Asian American Literary Criticism*, ed. Amy Ling and Shirley Lim (Philadelphia: Temple University Press, 1992). "Eugene O'Neill's *Marco Millions*: Desiring Marginality and the Dematerialization of Asia," originally published in Chinese, appears in English in *O'Neill in China*, ed. Lui Haiping and Leonard Swortzell (Westport, Connecticut: Greenwood Press, 1992). A shorter version of "Flawed Self-Representations: Authenticating Chinese American Marginality" appeared earlier as "David Henry Hwang's *M. Butterfly* and Philip Kan Gotanta's *Yankee Dawg You Die*: Repositioning Chinese American Marginality on the American Stage," *Theatre Journal* 42 (March 1990). And, finally I thank all who helped to make this book possible.

Marginal Sights

1 Introduction

Siting Race/Staging Chineseness

Here is madness elevated to spectacle above the silence of the asylums, and becoming a public scandal for the general delight. Unreason was hidden in the houses of confinement, but madness continued to be present on the stage of the world — with more commotion than ever.
— Michel Foucault

Since the beginning of the Western tradition in drama, dominant cultures have represented marginal or foreign racial groups in a manner that presents these characters as othered — that is, not only as different from people in the dominant culture but also as less than completely human or civilized. The Greeks, for example, had an all-purpose word for these people: barbarians. From Euripides' *Medea* through Shakespeare's *The Tempest* (as well as *Othello, The Merchant of Venice*, and even *Romeo and Juliet*) to O'Neill's *The Emperor Jones*, these characters, with few exceptions, have been cast negatively. Apparently they lack certain essential human qualities, and this condition of absence is often pivotal to the development of the dramatic conflict. It would seem, then, that the need to demean or dehumanize these othered people serves to maintain or reestablish an advantage for the dominant culture.

Playwrights and audiences alike have been fascinated with racial difference, and this fascination, though sometimes benign, has depended upon a process of fetishization. The constructed — allegedly fantastic — attributes ascribed to alien races identify them as creatures from distant lands, beyond the boundaries of civilization and normal existence. Often attached to the marginalized regions of the flat world, the circular *mappa mundi*, the inhabitants of these marginal pieces of geography were thought to be fantastic, monstrous beings. As constructed beings without a real presence, they could not argue against their marginalization. And, as Aristotle had noted, beings living beyond the reaches of known governmental structures, without the state, were either gods or beasts.[1] Obviously not gods, those living beyond the known Eurocentric notions of state had to be beasts. By the Middle Ages, these beings were often graphically represented without heads, with crane-like necks, ill-proportioned or misdirected feet, animal faces, and with faces imbedded in chests.

These beasts were simply accepted as the exotic creatures which God, as reconstituted in the Judeo-Christian form, had created to dwell in paradise situated in the East: "And the Lord God planted a garden eastward in Eden."[2] The Hereford *Mappa Mundi* (1280), typical of the circular "T and O" maps of the era, locates the "East," or Asia, at the top of the flat circular world, with Europe and Africa each occupying half of the lower section. Surrounded by Asia, Jerusalem, source of both antiquity and Christianity, occupies the center. Such maps often displayed the monstrous races residing on the edges of this world, which feathered out into mystery, far from the centrality of governments.

Rudolf Wittkower, tracing the history of the monstrous races inhabiting these mystical sites on the margins of the known world, noted that many explorers of the fourteenth and fifteenth centuries believed that they had "located Paradise" in their travels. "Friar Jordanus placed it between the 'terza India' and Ethiopia, John of Marignola believed it to be in Ceylon, Odoric of Pordenone found it 50 days west of Cathay, John of Hese on a mythical journey professed to have reached it in the extreme East; and Columbus, who thought to his death that he had discovered the sea route to India, was convinced that he had passed near it."[3]

During the European Renaissance, however, the world was radically refigured from a flat tabletop into a sphere now fixed in proper perspective by a grid of meridians. This change in understanding at once problematized the location of these mystical places. Indeed, as Asia became merely a part of the world, Europe redefined itself as the center, with optical perspective providing both agency and superstructure. In the process Asia ceased to be the site of ancient wisdom and became just another — or, more to the point, an othered — location.

Still, received knowledge influenced the observations of explorers such as Jordanus, Marignola, Odoric, and later Mandeville, who claimed to have come in contact with races fitting the medieval descriptions of monsters.[4] The tension between reality and the monstrous of imaginary realms produced some amusing ruptures in the social text of Renaissance Italy. Christian entrepreneurs, with worker populations devastated by plague, were allowed to import slaves, but only if they were heathen. Because Asians and other people of color lived beyond the boundaries of a Eurocentric perspective, they qualified as heathens. Imported by the thousands, these slaves *de genere Tartarorum* worked regularly in the homes of the most conspicuous families of Florence. They were "rapidly absorbed by the indigenous population, [and] a certain Mongolian strain would not have been rare in Tuscan homes and streets." Indeed, the introduction of these Asian slaves significantly altered the demographics of Tuscany. One study notes that "among the 7,534 infants delivered, between 1394 and 1485, in the Florentine foundling hospital, up to 32 per cent were illegitimate children of those oriental slaves. When recognized, these halfbreeds followed the condition of the father and were declared free by law."[5] Once declared free by law, they likely ceased to be beasts.

This type of interaction, often producing offspring, humanized the Asian and other alien races. Accordingly, it is puzzling to find that even in the sixteenth century, with the continued trade in slaves from all over the known world, Cardinal Ippolito de' Medici (1511–1535) maintained a human menagerie of

barbarians who talked no less than twenty different languages, and who were all of them perfect specimens of their races. Among them were incomparable *voltigeurs* of the best blood of the North African

Moors, Tartar bowmen, Negro wrestlers, Indian divers, and Turks, who generally accompanied the Cardinal on his hunting expeditions. When he was overtaken by an early death (1535), this motley band carried the corpse on their shoulders from Itri to Rome, and mingled with the general mourning for the open-handed Cardinal their medley of tongues and violent gesticulations.[6]

It would seem that the Renaissance mind, though prepared on some occasions to grant humanity to others, preferred to cling to the imaginary construction of the alien slave as monstrous. Though obviously not beasts, these foreigners, because they lived by extra-European laws, were othered by European xenophobia. Moreover, Ippolito de' Medici likely employed the museum strategy of the survey collection to affirm his position of power. His control over each individual in the panoptic survey apparently doubled as an articulation of authority over the homeland of each representative. Thus the racial other was enslaved even as the paternalistic Christian desire to civilize the heathen emerged.

Perhaps Europe's most significant early social contribution to America was a two-thousand-year-old Eurocentric prejudice that maintained the bestial representation of those not fitting into familiar governmental structures. Well before Asians began to appear in America, the framework that would provide for their representation had been established. The Chinese, and Asians in general, first appear as representational issues during the nineteenth century, their constructed images emerging amidst a rapidly expanding world of visual text. But the constructed aspects of Asianness which survive today appear stripped of the nineteenth-century intertextual relationships which provided definition and initially enforced visibility. This Asianness, kept in place by the power of the desire for domination which brought it into view but now drained of its substance, stands available for continual refiguration. Rendered a blank, the Asian in late twentieth-century America is a void waiting to be refilled. Of course, the Euro-American advantage in the deployment of the constructed stereotype is that one never need interact with the real and can misinterpret as one pleases. But all are victims of this position. Americans visiting Asia are often disappointed, noting that indeed

Asians in American Chinatowns, J-Towns, Little Saigons, or the constructed habitats of Epcot Center seem more authentic, and cleaner too — a sad commentary on the extent to which Asians in America, like those in the sex shops of Bangkok, have become complicitous with the colonial gaze, and on how that way of looking has shaped Anglo expectations as well. The continuing late twentieth-century commodification of such examples of constructed Asian American sites, constantly consumed by white America, articulates the power this history has over both populations and serves as a reminder that Asian America never existed beyond the already represented stereotype bestowed upon it.

Displacing nineteenth-century stereotypes has proved especially difficult for Asian Americans. An attack is often little more than an assault on an empty shell whose substance was long ago drained but whose current existence seems more persuasive because of the new attention given to it. Still, to ignore the stereotype is to leave the geography littered with awkward figurations of Asianness that recall a bitter past which continues to affect the present in subtle ways.

Those who rail against the dominant culture's imaging of Asians in America have tended to reinforce images of exoticism by focusing, for instance, on details of costume.[7] The Lotus Blossom stereotype, for example, is attacked, but without naming the rupture through which this representation was forced into visibility. Lost in some mystical moment of spontaneous generation, Lotus Blossom seems to assume an almost folkloric right to continue. And, what of the seriocomic Chinese detective, Charlie Chan, whose offspring desire to be American but fail, and in their failure reinscribe more deeply the father's foreignness? Competent Asian American parents, then, are disfigured as their progeny are denied a place in the representational West. The failure to adequately identify and interrogate such moments gives the stereotype an almost authoritative sense of rightful social construction.

This extended essay, then, seeks to interact with a few of these moments. The study consists of ten readings, each a treatment of Euro-American strategies deployed in the staging of the Chinese in America. While the focus is on the Chinese, the implications for the American staging of marginalized people in general should be clear. Moreover, the study focuses as much on the *sites* as on the constructed representation, for the representation reaches out to construct and reinscribe itself before and within the spectator. The objective is not to construct a comprehensive account of the Chinese or Asian stereotype with suggestions for how to respond, but rather through the readings to bring Asian America "nearer to the roots of our oppression"[8] and to contribute to the dismantling of the apparatus which enforces Asian American invisibility.

2

The Panoptic Empire of the Gaze

Authenticity and the Touristic Siting of Chinese America

The earth was made for Dombey and Son to trade in, and the sun and moon were made to give them light. Rivers and seas were formed to float their ships; rainbows gave them promise of fair weather; winds blew for or against their enterprises; stars and planets circled in their orbits, to preserve inviolate a system of which they were the centre.
— Charles Dickens

The bourgeois dream of empire, expressed ironically by Dickens in his novel *Dombey and Son* (1848), was taken for granted by most late nineteenth-century writers and so thoroughly imbued the Western psyche that such great expectations seemed natural. It is within this context that the department of knowledge called anthropology came into existence during the nineteenth century as an enterprise in which white men fanned out across the world to look at and "study" people of color. The anthropological gaze emerged as the mechanism by which the common man came to participate in national dreams of empire.

While postcolonial nineteenth-century America had not achieved the extraterritorial empire of its European counterparts, the desire for an imperialist perspective was manifest in American institutions of the day. America had inherited a governmental tradition that featured genocide and the internal colonization of native American lands. Further, the military solution of the native American problem created labor shortages that led to the importation of black

slaves. The imperialist perspective of early America would have a significant impact on the representation of othered populations.

Of interest here is the effect this perspective had on the construction
of Chineseness in the representational practice of the period and the subsequent creation of new sites for the reinscription of this Chineseness
across broad ranges of spectatorship. The evolution of the anthropological gaze, then, is central. For, while denying overt connection with
empire, it nonetheless allowed America to claim equal status in the community of imperialistic Western powers, but under the sign of altruism.
In turn this altruistic anthropological desire enslaved the Asian subject
to yield a stage character befitting the imperialistic gaze, now reconstituted as American.

By the middle of the nineteenth century two forms of the empowering
gaze become clear, the serial and the voyeuristic. The popular form of
the serial, or survey, offered amusements which brought together apparently authoritative series and collocations of objects to create the *potential* for meaning. Panoptic in sensibility and usually nonnarrative, these
entertainments employed displacement as a structural force and included museum displays, vaudeville, circus, travelogues, and even melo-
drama. The potency of this mode of production lay in its ability to oblit-
erate geography and narrative time, in the process offering the spectator
an almost godlike option to either examine with care or completely ignore the efforts up on stage. While these popular forms offered the possibility for significance, nothing would come of it. Producers preferred
to use this potential as little more than a false proairetic to fascinate audiences while entrapping them for future exploitation. The voyeuristic
gaze, generally associated with the emergent self-conscious literary elite
of mid-nineteenth-century narrative realism, served to affirm the authority of the looker, generally at the expense of the object — which in
turn was often reduced to stereotype.

Both ways of looking — the serial and the voyeuristic — operated to
reinforce a particular institutional culture of the gaze, each limited to its
own audience. The serial offered an amusingly empowering yet dismis-
sive gaze to entertain the masses, while the voyeuristic gaze offered exquisitely fashioned, fetishized "realistic" visions of everyday life which

could inspire polite conversation for the learned elite. Significantly, each of these forms produced stereotypical racial representations while promising an authentic experience.

Chineseness first appeared in America within the displacing structure of the variety stage. For instance, Voltaire's *Orphan of China* (1755), adapted into English by Arthur Murphy, appeared in Philadelphia's Southwark Theatre on 16 January 1767. This production, like the premiere, presented Middle Eastern dress in a vaguely "Oriental" mode of representation. Still, this exotic construction was likely the first performance of Chineseness to make its way to what would become the American stage. Indeed, the notion of Chineseness under the sign of the exotic became familiar to the American spectator long before sightings of the actual Chinese. In 1781, a "Chinese Umbra" display, or shadow performance, was described thus: "This evening will be exhibited At the sign of the Store-grate, nearly opposite the Coffee-House, and next to the Hessian guard-house, The Chinese Umbra, On an entire new construction; with a variety of devices, in lively colours, such as ships sailing on the water, a representation of the sun and moon, with a view of Noah's Ark. . . ."[1] "Chinese Shades," or shadow displays, were popular throughout the last decades of the eighteenth century and were frequently featured in benefit performances. The novelty of the shadow performance would sometimes be combined with live action, as in a 1789 "transparent scene — Les Ombres Chinoises — in which will be introduced a very entertaining and laughable Scene between the Coblers, Barbers, Taylors, &c."[2] Typically, these novelty pieces of exotic display were part of a larger proairetic sequence:

At No. 14, William street, in a room adjacent to where the Speaking figure is exhibited, will be opened with An Introductory Prologue, After which will be presented, an exhibition of Mechanical Artificers in the Chinese Shades . . . A Sailor's Prologue. A Pantomimical Representation, in the Italian Shades, of Robinson Crusoe, With transparent scenes adapted, taken from Cook's Voyage. A representation of the Broken Bridge and Drunken Carpenter. With a view of Pasaic Falls. A favorite Hunting scene, with SONGS adapted. The whole to conclude with Bucks have at ye all, And a view of Broad Way from St. Paul's, in Transparency.[3]

And, indeed, on 13 July 1796, a "Chinese Shades" production at Ricketts's Circus in New York promised six actors performing "as Chinese" and a representation of a "Grand Chinese Temple" for the finale.[4]

While it is clear from the cast list for the circus performance that the portrayals of the Chinese were executed by non-Asian performers, an 1808 performance by the Pepin and Breschard circus troupe in New York offers "THE YOUNG CHINESE" who "will display a variety of Comic attitudes and Vaultings, over his Horse in full speed." While it is not clear from the cast list of this troupe that the individual advertised was truly Asian, it should be noted that his appearance seems part of an increased use of racial representation, for along with the "Young Chinese" the program promised circus performances by a "Young African," as well as characters with Spanish- and French-sounding surnames.[5]

From the outset, then, the Chinese in America resided solely in the province of the imaginary. Indeed, the consistency of the representation of Chineseness is astonishing. For example, a review of *A Chinese Honeymoon* (1902), a musical comedy, some one hundred years later notes: "The piece is only another variation of a senseless species of stage entertainment, plotless and formless, that has become popular of recent years, which is neither drama, comedy nor operetta, and defies all intelligent criticism. It is really vaudeville with the various 'acts' strung on the slenderest possible plot . . . The stage settings and costumes are as beautiful as have ever been seen in this city . . . the Chinese gowns constitute a perfect orgy of splendid coloring."[6] The Chinese appeared in fleeting moments within a longer sequence of performances designed to provide the spectator with a pleasant sense of plentitude, but devoid of narrative. This deployment of Chineseness, at once in the service of both the survey and the exotic, marks its place in the imaginary realm of American experience to this day. (The 1992 program for the Ringling Brothers, Barnum and Bailey Circus remains full of Chinese and Mongolian performers who are presented as exotic.) The early use of the Orient is in keeping with what could be called an Anglo-American desire to define

| LORD HIGH ADMIRAL | THE EMPEROR | LORD CHANCELLOR |
| (William Pruette) | (Edwin Stevens) | (William Burress) |

"A CHINESE HONEYMOON" AT THE CASINO

Americanness by noting difference, especially racial. This theatricalization of difference emerged of necessity, out of the need to justify the extermination of native Americans and the institution of slavery.

As dreams of American empire in a liberal tradition developed, previously popular entertainments were often turned into projects which promised scientific knowledge through careful study. This tendency is perhaps most evident in the enterprise of the museum as large-scale *Wunderkammer* for the display of souvenirs of colonial expansion.[7] One of the most famous of the early American museums, Barnum's, offered little more than collections of freakish novelties gathered from around the world. Displayed within the cases were collections of dead things which in real life would never have been caught dead together. These objects were sufficiently fascinating to lure audiences back for return visits, especially as the museum offered the continuing promise of more oddities the next time.

In 1834 a "Chinese Lady" named Afong Moy was offered to the public gaze at the American Museum in New York City. Moy's performances of Chineseness were usually part of events which at various times included the likes of "a party of Indians . . . to dance and hold a council . . . Schweighoffer, the magician . . . Finn, the glassblower . . . Canadian dwarfs, 30 and 32 inches high, respectively . . . Potter in Grecian exercises, and fifty automaton figures at work."[8] Often displayed in "native costume," Moy, along with "Harrington, the magician," once found herself inserted into a performance of "Euterpean Hall Sinclair's Peristrephis, or moving panorama from Spring Garden, London, a moving picture of the Battle and the Village of Waterloo," offered at the City Saloon in 1835.[9] Exactly how a "Chinese Lady" and a magician figured in the Battle of Waterloo is unclear, but the display, which also featured four dioramas, would certainly suggest a lack of interest in traditional narrative. Moy along with the magician and the four dioramas combined for a grand panoptic event which no doubt offered to the gaze of the spectator a sense of empowerment as important historic moments and diversions collapsed into scenes created exclusively for the sake of audience amusement. Between 1834 and 1837, Moy performed her Chineseness at several locations, including the American Museum, Peale's Museum (which would later be purchased by P. T. Barnum), an unnamed venue located at 8 Park Place, the Brooklyn Institute, and the City Saloon. By late 1837, perhaps tiring of performing Chineseness, the Chinese Lady was reported "waiting for a ship to China."[10] A contemporary print dated 1835 seems to suggest that Moy's displays included an appropriate chinoiserie setting.[11] From the lithograph it seems that the simple foreignness of Afong Moy was deemed sufficient novelty to warrant her display. Likewise, beginning in the 1830s, P. T. Barnum's displays of the "Siamese Twins," Chang and Eng,[12] the most famous stage display of Asianness in the nineteenth century, further contributed

Afong Moy. Museum of the City of New York.

to the institutionalization of Chinese racial representation as appropriate for museum or freak show display.

The context for this type of display is the anthropological gaze associated with modern museums, in which the power and authority of the spectator's privileged look is affirmed, usually at the expense of the novel

A Chinese family on display. Museum of the City of New York.

"primitive" objectified or dead Other. Thus, while little significant meaning could be discerned, the spectators still could become "master of all they survey." As museums assumed a more pseudoscientific anthropological stance, audiences came not merely to look as one might survey a circus sideshow, but to study, to learn, to participate in an exchange which promised an authentic, scientifically grounded explication of the freakish assembled objects, despite the awkward truncation of time and geography.

Representations of Chineseness continued in the great "ethnographic congresses" of the variety and circus stages during the 1880s and 1890s. In 1884, for example, the Barnum and London Shows promised to display "Chang, Chinese Giant and Tallest Man in the World," along with "40 Trained Elephants, 50 Cages of Rare Animals, 16 Wide Open Dens of Wild Beasts, 80 Remarkable, Bewildering, Amazing and Sensational

Acts by 300 Star Performers [including] General Dot, the Orator, Actor and Dude Clown. Major Atom, the Elf of the Human Race. Fat Women, Male and Female Living Skeletons, Bearded Women, Wild Children, Tattooed Martyrs, Pallid Moors, Midgets, Dwarfs, Giants, and all the Museum Sights Worth Seeing." Beyond this, the ethnological congress also promised "Savage and Barbarous Tribes, embracing Pagans, Heathens, Sun-Worshipers and unschooled People from remote countries barely mentioned in history. 100 Rude and Revengeful Barbarians, Believing in Female Polygamy, Followers of the False Prophet, 'El Mahdi,' Conjurors, Sorcerers and Superstitious Savages"—all this under the banner of the "Only Show Which Exhibits All that It Advertises."[13] Not to be outdone by the likes of Barnum, Robinson's Mammoth Dime Museum and Theatre of New Orleans reasoned that if Barnum could offer a Chinese giant, then they could display "Che-Mah, the Chinese Dwarf." Accompanying Che-Mah in the "Museum Department" were various freaks:

> The Living Skeleton, John W. Coffey. The Spotted Man, Old Ike. The Three Atoms, The Denver Midgets. The Tattooed Man, Frank DeBurdg. The Elastic Shouldered man, Frank Clark. The Largest Lady in the World, Mme. June. Curious beyond Description, The Texas Camel Ox. The Tattooed Circassian Prince, Mons. Osmon. Wonderful Automaton representing the Mechanics' Dream. Punch and Judy for the Children. Troop of Bohemian Glass Blowers, etc.[14]

One might assume that Che-Mah would get lost in the chaos of these competing museum attractions, but an illustration published with the advertisement for the event suggests that the producers designed a situation which would assure something of a fetish value for his appearance.

Beyond the pure anthropological display of otherness, Asian stage representations began to appear in theatrical texts beginning in the second half of the nineteenth century. These generally offered a neutralized Asian character — usually Chinese male — in some comic form. The methods employed in the disfigurement of this type of Asian character are significant and were doubtless wildly entertaining to Anglo-Ameri-

The Resort for Ladies and Children.

ROBINSON'S

Mammoth Dime Museum & Theatre

126 CANAL STREET,

EUGENE ROBINSON..............................MANAGER.

THURSDAY, OCTOBER 30, AT 10 A. M.

GRAND OPENING..............................GREAT BANGLE DAY

EVERY LADY, EVERY GIRL, EVERY GIRL BABY,
Visiting the Museum on the opening day will be presented with a
SOUVENIR ONE DIME BANGLE.
READ THE LIST OF OUR MAMMOTH DOUBLE COMPANY.

MUSEUM DEPARTMENT.

The Chinese Dwarf, **Che-Mah.**

The Living Skeleton, **John W. Coffey.**

The Spotted Man, **Old Ike.**

The Three Atoms, **The Denver Midgets.**

The Tattooed Man, **Frank De Burdg.**

The Elastic Shouldered man, **Frank Clark.**

The Largest Lady in the World, **Mme. June.**

Curious Beyond Description, **The Texas Camel Ox.**

The Tattooed Circassian Prince, **Mons. Osmon.**

Wonderful Automaton representing the **Mechanics' Dream.**

Punch and Judy for the Children.

Troop of **Bohemian Glass Blowers, etc.**

STAGE PERFORMANCE in the Beautiful Theatorium EVERY HOUR by the following well known artists:

MISS MARTHA E. STEEN, the justly styled Empress of Mediums, and Second Sight-Seer, Mind Reader and Second Sight-Lightning Calculator, assisted by **PROF. CHAS. E. STEEN,** the East India Illusionist and Card Manipulator.

MRS. and MISS SAGE, in their beautiful selections on the Musical Glasses.

LITTLE JESSIE PARKES in Violin and Serio-Comic Specialties.

MR. GUS HARCOURT, German Dialect Comedian, in his specialty act in which he stands pre-eminent.

HOON FAMILY in their Refined Instrumental and Vocal Specialties.

MISS CARRIE ST. LEON in Operatic Ballads.

Ladies can visit the Museum without an escort, and Children can come alone. We aim to please, instruct and entertain. A Giant Show at Midget Prices. Doors open from 10 a. m. to 10 p. m. **Remember, One Dime Admits to a 1—One Dime.**

1884 advertisement for Che-Mah. Circus World Museum, State Historical Society of Wisconsin.

can audiences of the nineteenth century. James J. McCloskey's *Across the Continent; Or Scenes From New York Life and the Pacific Railroad* (1870) is a clear example of the survey, in this case a travelogue, which compressed geography and featured ethnic, including Chinese, stereotyping. Employing a loose narrative structure whose real function was to provide a clothesline for the display of various ethnic types, *Across the Continent* made no claim to authenticity in its representations. Italians were hot-blooded, Irish always drunk, and the Chinese incapable of understanding:

CHI. [*Runs up to her*] You like some ricee — [*Aunt Susannah turns back on him. . . . Sits down and takes drink out of bottle*]

CHI. Ah ha — Melican woman like jig water. Me likee, too. [*Takes bottle of water out of her hand and drinks. Offers it back several times, but fools her and drinks himself, talking Chinese all the time, and keeps this up till the bottle is empty*] Me makee mashee. [*Sits beside her*] Ah, there my sizee — me stealee you. [*Tries to put his arm around her. She jumps quickly — he falls, then chases her*]

JOE. Here — what is the matter Tart?

CHI. [*Joe comes forward with Tom*] Melican woman fightee.

JOE. Come here, Tart. [*To others*] Watch me telephone to China. [*Takes Tart's cue*] Hello, Tart!

CHI. Hello!

JOE. You're crazy.

CHI. Me, too [*Joe turns away laughing*] Now me talkee. [*Takes end of cue*] Hello — hello — hello — [*Jerks his cue disgusted — jumps on box*][15]

The resulting new voyeuristic-serial transcended the expectations of its previously separate audiences. The alien look of the Chinese when animated and inserted into a narrative in which the practice of survey could operate created a new gaze with the potential for a persuasive sense of authenticity.

While McCloskey did not claim to present authentic Chineseness, others did. Bret Harte and Mark Twain's Asian character in *Ah Sin* (1877) purported to offer "as good and as natural and consistent a Chinaman as he could see in San Francisco. . . . Therefore it seems well enough to let the public study him a little on the stage . . . "[16] Bret Harte and Mark Twain could claim authenticity for their Ah Sin character by virtue of their actual exposure to the Chinese living in California. In the service of their claim of authenticity, they employed the museum strategy of enumerating differences between the Chinese and Americans, thereby creating a character who existed as little more than a personification of collocated aspects of cultural difference. But their representation was clearly fabricated to meet the expectations of their East Coast audiences, and such fabrication eventually replaced all other notions of Chineseness. Once this "authentic" frontier notion of the Chinese was established, new more engaging forms had to be invented. Typical of these was Eugene O'Neill's *Marco Millions* (1927). As *Ah Sin* was intended to offer a favorable view of the Chinese on the Western frontier, so O'Neill hoped to contrast favorably the mysterious wisdom of his Orient with the materialist tendencies of the West. Good intentions aside, O'Neill could do little better than reinscribe the imperialist vision of an impotent romantic Orient whose wisdom fails when confronted by the power of the monied West. Still, the work is remarkable because O'Neill, who had yet to visit Asia, saw fit to locate the play in an imaginary China in which the Italian entourage often resembles tourists. This reinscription of the travelogue by a prominent literary figure affords the play yet another kind of authenticity, while also validating an imperialist, touristic view of Asianness, and indeed the world as a whole.

Such displacing, touristic perspectives of Asianness were immediately inscribed into the popular cinematic and photographic texts of the early twentieth century. Snapshots and films of San Francisco's Chinatown became staged representations of the Chinese in America. Indeed, to this day, films like *Chinatown* (1974) and *Big Trouble in Little China* (1986) continually rehearse the notion of a dark, exotic site where, like a traveler in a foreign land, one seeks fleeting adventures. These impressions, despite their snapshot quality, disclose an anthropological desire to articulate dominance over previous notions of the subject, now rendered naive by a still greater "authenticity." This almost erotic "over-investment" in seeing the Chinese has been eloquently noted in Rey Chow's recent treatment of Bertolucci's *The Last Emperor* (1987):

Of all the components of this "over-investment," the most obvious are, of course, the visual elements of a re-created Imperial China, the exotic architecture, the abundance of art objects, the clothes worn by the members of the late Manchu court, their peculiar mannerisms, the camel or two resting on the outskirts of the Forbidden City, and the thousands of servants at the service of the Emperor. The endowment of museum quality on the filmic images feeds the craving of the eyes. The cinematic audience become vicarious tourists in front of "China" whom is served on a screen.[17]

The commodification of this anthropologically authentic notion of Chineseness, continually reinscribed, has dominated to the extent that even recent well-intentioned liberal theatre practitioners such as Montreal's Theatre Repère could not avoid reinscribing the stereotype in what has been hailed as their masterwork, *The Dragons' Trilogy* (1989).[18] Stridently avant-garde in its ambitious desire to show significances in Asian Canadian and Anglo-Canadian relationships, *The Dragons' Trilogy*, spanning three generations in Canadian history, had a running time of some six hours and used over two tons of sand in an elegant set which provided a fascinating grounding for its portrayal of race relations in troubled times. Director Robert Lepage consciously sought to break with stereotypical portrayals of Chineseness while pursuing greater authenticity through an experimental mode of production. Unfortunately, he too fell into the trap of attacking the stereotype while unwittingly reinscribing it. Despite the kindness and good will shown by the Chinese son, his father (an old laundryman) is portrayed as the untrustworthy gambler who is not above taking a woman as part of a stake in a poker game. The laundryman's sisters are literally faceless: they perform with stockings over their faces and seek only to dig the hole that will allow them to tunnel back to China. The myth of the sojourner Chinese whose only desire is to return to China is long dead. Likewise, the Chinese son's selfless, blind willingness to take care of another man's red-haired daughter as his own recalls the impotent, and therefore nonthreatening, "Chink" of D. W. Griffith's *Broken Blossoms* (original title, *The Chink and the Child*, 1919).

Scene from The Dragons' Trilogy. *International Theatre Festival of Chicago.*

It is this "authentic" commodified vision of Chineseness, and its history, that recent Asian American playwrights have sought to displace. Unfortunately for Asian America, most recent playwrights have located the struggle under the sign of greater *racial* authenticity. What better way to get behind the facade of the Chinese stereotype than to have a Chinese American guide? Still, the subjugation and commodification of representations of Asian otherness has such a long history that Asian American playwrights raised in this tradition are left with little space for the creation of anything other than compounded stereotypes for popular consumption. For example, despite the popularity of both David Henry Hwang's *M. Butterfly* (1988) and Philip Kan Gotonda's *Yankee Dawg You Die* (1988), an awkward tension existed between the Anglo-American audiences' desire to see authenticated stereotypes on the stage and the writers' desire to create "real" representations that are commercially viable. While their attacks on the dominant culture's stereotypes were well intentioned, to be successful they finally had to offer what amounted to little more than refigured but "authentic" reinscriptions. In yielding to

7 Faces of Dr. Lao. *Wisconsin Center for Film and Theatre Research, State Historical Society of Wisconsin.*

consumer desires, their attacks not only proved impotent, but their plays contributed to the creation of a new order of authenticated stereotype.

Clearly, the tension between Asian American desire for identity and marketplace forces creates the possibility for confusion. In the *7 Faces of Dr. Lao* (1964), a white man, playing a Chinaman who impersonates legendary European figures, saves the town of Abalone from its own greed. Dr. Lao (Tony Randall), a mystical, aphorism-spouting Chinese fakir, arrives in the turn-of-the-century frontier town to stage an Oriental circus. During the course of his one-man circus he impersonates important mythological figures while declaring the "whole world is a circus . . . part of the circus of Dr. Lao." As the Chinese hero leaves the now radically altered town, the bewildered inhabitants ask: "I wonder where he came from . . . or, where he's going . . . or, if he was ever here at all." Indeed, such is the contested terrain in which Asian American representation must reside. For while it is not clear that the Chinaman as constituted in the popular consciousness ever really existed, the stereotype remembered somehow seems to have taken on a life of its own.

3

Bret Harte and Mark Twain's *Ah Sin*

Locating China in the Geography of the American West

Whoever sees Mr. Parsloe [the actor] *in this* [dramatic] *piece sees as good and as natural and consistent a Chinaman as he could see in San Francisco. I think his portrayal of the character* [of Ah Sin] *reaches perfection. . . . The Chinaman is going to become a very frequent spectacle all over America, by and by, and a difficult political problem, too. Therefore it seems well enough to let the public study him a little on the stage beforehand.*
— Mark Twain

In the nineteenth century, an emerging post-colonial America struggled desperately for a sense of national identity. Toward this end American writers often contrasted the national idiosyncrasies of its most recent immigrant population with those of the more established American community. This was particularly true of the popular theatre of the day, which tended to hold representations of the latest immigrant group up for ridicule. The process of comparison had a socializing effect on the incoming European immigrant population because its members, viewing the stereotypical representations on stage, could laugh at and deny any connection with the garish characterizations while affirming their new allegiance to America. Accordingly, the British, the French, the German, the Irish, and the Italian were each in turn subjects for viciously humorous attacks before receding into the background to later emerge as central characters on the American stage.

Not all writers, however, offered up stereotypes. Some, self-consciously literary, attempted to offer democratically even-handed, finely drawn characterizations of both fully assimilated Americans and recently landed foreigners. Rarely did these two opposing tendencies — the popular and the literary — intersect. Bret Harte and Mark Twain's *Ah Sin* (1877) provides insight into one moment in which these two trajectories did intersect to create a space for representations of the Chinese in the geography of America's Western states.

As most scholars will readily agree, both Mark Twain (Samuel L. Clemens, 1835–1910) and Bret Harte (1836–1902) are remembered as writers whose works display an apparently heartfelt desire for accurate portrayals of life on America's Western frontier.[1] The emergence of a play, especially by the likes of Mark Twain and Bret Harte, with a Chinese character in the title role would seem to suggest the assimilation of the Chinese into the mainstream of American life. From the outset it becomes all too obvious that this is not the case. While it is not entirely clear why the representation of the Chinese character does not follow the pattern of other ethnic immigrant populations on the American stage, an interrogation of the tensions which define the presence of the Chinese character should result in a deeper understanding of the position of the Chinese on America's Western frontier.

Ah Sin opened in New York at Daly's Fifth Avenue Theatre on 31 July 1877, after preview performances at the National Theatre in Washington D.C.[2] The plot is typically melodramatic, working to fulfill the expectations of late nineteenth-century American audiences. Both the *New York Times* and *The World* of 1 August 1877 printed generally favorable reviews of the piece. The *Times* review offered the following summary of the plot:

> It turns upon the rascality of one Broderick who all but murders Bill Plunkett — the champion liar of Calaveras — and then accuses York, a "gentleman miner" of the crime. Just as a committee of lynchers are about to act upon a verdict of guilty, Ah Sin fastens the guilt of the deed upon Broderick by the exhibition of the murderer's coat which Broderick thought he had long since done away with and Plunkett

DALY'S

5th Av  Theatre

PROPRIETOR AND MANAGER...Mr. AUGUSTIN DALY

Tuesday Night, July 31st, 1877,

Mr. DALY will begin his NINTH SEASON with the production of a DRAMATIC WORK, in four acts, by

MARK TWAIN and BRET HARTE,

Written expressly for MR. C. T. PARSLOE, and entitled

"A H   S I N !"

In which

MR. PARSLOE

will appear in his GREAT and ORIGINAL CREATION of

THE HEATHEN CHINEE.

The drama has been produced under the immediate supervision of Mark Twain, and will be presented with entirely New Scenery from Local Sketches, by Mr. Witham and Mr. Thompson, and interpreted by A Specially Selected Company, which will be seen in the following

CAST:

SHIRLEY TEMPEST, a San Francisco Belle, and Heiress of an adventurous spirit..Miss DORA GOLDTHWAITE
(Her first appearance here.)

Mrs. TEMPEST, the Fashionable and Fastidious Mother of the above young lady.....Miss MARY WELLS

Mrs. PLUNKETT, the too apparent cause of Mr. Plunkett's absence from home......Mrs. G. H. GILBERT

CAROLINE ANASTASIA PLUNKETT, Practical Daughter of an Impractical Parent...Miss EDITH BLANDE
(From the Gaiety and Criterion Theatres, London.)

YORK, the Gentleman Miner and Owner of the "40 Mill"...........................Mr. HENRY CRISP

BRODERICK, a Knave through circumstances over which he *ought* to have control.
....Mr. EDMUND COLLIER

BILL PLUNKETT, "Uncle Billy," the Champion Liar of Calaveras...............Mr. P. A. ANDERSON
(His first appearance here.)

JUDGE TEMPEST, a wealthy and retired Lawyer, with an Interest in the Mines and in one of the Miners..... ....Mr. H. A. WEAVER
(His first appearance here.)

FERGUSON, Foreman of the "Keystone" Mine and Chief of the "Vigilantes".....Mr. WM. DAVIDGE

MASTERS, Foreman of the "Heart's Delight," and another of the lawless society of law and order..Mr. E. VARREY
(His first appearance here.)

BOSTON, one more of the same sort..Mr. VINING BOWERS

JAKE MILLER, ditto..Mr. F. M. CHAPMAN

Miners, Jurymen, &c., &c.

Act I..Scene—Plunkett's Cabin on the Stanislaus (Witham). The Stained Jacket! Ah Sin makes a Profitable Sale.

Act II..Scene—AH SIN'S LAUNDRY! (Thompson.) An Exchange of Names and a Confusion of Identities. Miss Tempest makes a Conquest, and the Vigilantes make an Attack, while Ah Sin makes a Novel Defence!

Act III..Scene—York's Cottage (Thompson and Roberts). Ah Sin Leaves his Duties. The Heiress is Conquered and York is Captured—twice. Last time somewhat unpleasantly, and Ah Sin takes a hand in all around.

Act IV..Scene 1—A Roadside. The Heiress makes an Appeal and the Judge Closes his Heart.
Scene 2—JUDGE LYNCH'S COURT. The Trial in Progress, and York's Fate is Decided by a Border Jury. Ah Sin's Jacket Decides the Verdict, and the Skeleton of his Cabin Decides the Day.

First Matinee of "Ah Sin"

Saturday, August 4th, at 2 o'clock.

being subsequently brought into court safe and sound, the piece terminates happily.[3]

Significantly, while the title of the play is *Ah Sin*, it is clear from the plot summary that the title character serves not as a lead but merely as a plot-advancing device toward the end of the play. The character Ah Sin enters the text with much fanfare. But his entrance is almost unnoticed because he appears between major sweeps of narrative which establish Plunkett's position and Broderick's villainy.[4] Ah Sin, then, at this moment in the text exists merely as a disruption in the narrative, serving as a mechanism for displacing or deflecting any potentially serious content. He next appears as an unacknowledged presence when he secretly contrives to predetermine the outcome of a poker game in favor of his master (19–22). In his first nonpassive appearance in the play, Ah Sin agrees to actions which place him on the wrong side of the law (24–26). While continually subjected to physical abuse, Ah Sin is treated with contempt as Broderick calls him a "slant eyed son of the yellow jaunders. . . . you jabbering idiot. . . . you moral cancer, you unsolvable political problem" (10–11, 87).

A marginal and substandard character, Ah Sin is placed in a secondary dramatic position that is reinforced throughout the piece. Miss Tempest describes him almost endearingly as one might describe a pet: "Don't mind him — don't be afraid. . . . Poor Ah Sin is harmless — only a little ignorant and awkward." Mrs. Tempest complains that "when he shakes his head it makes me nervous to hear his dried faculties rattle." Indeed, as a "poor dumb animal, with his tail on top of his head instead of where it ought to be," Ah Sin, as Mrs. Tempest states, is capable of at best mere imitation: "Well upon my word, this mental vacuum is a Chinaman to the marrow in one thing — the monkey faculty of imitating" (52–53). His lack of comprehension of American ways coupled with his desire to learn through imitation cause Ah Sin to fall victim to much comic business. When Mrs. Tempest drops a plate while setting the table, Ah Sin follows her lead and shatters a whole set of dinnerware (52).[5] Similarly, his inability to grasp American vernacular produces a comic situation when he is asked to show what he "picked up" while attending the theatre. Instead of singing the song he learned, Ah Sin displays the bric-a-brac he picked up from the floor of the theatre (68).

Yet despite Judge Tempest's comment that "the imperturbability of these Chinamen is insufferable" (33), it is not clear that this Chinese sought to be cast in the role of Other. Indeed, Ah Sin seeks continually to blend in. But in scenes of general conviviality when all present would shake hands, Ah Sin extends his only to be spurned (86), and when he speaks, all eyes in the silent room turn to him as if to question his right to participate (83–84).[6] Still, Mark Twain proclaimed that "whoever sees Mr. Parsloe in this piece sees as good and as natural and consistent a Chinaman as he could see in San Francisco. I think his portrayal of the character reaches perfection."[7] Generally speaking, newspaper critics of the day agreed with Mark Twain's assessment. One of these papers, however, called Ah Sin "a contemptible thief and an imperturbable liar."[8]

This constitution of the Chinese as a marginal Other mirrors the identity that the American public created for and enforced upon the Chinese. Ah Sin reminds us that "Chinaman evidence no good" (69, 88), and indeed since 1854 the Chinese had been forbidden the right to testify against whites in California courts of law.[9] Even the Burlingame Treaty of 1868, which allowed open immigration, denied the Chinese the right to become American citizens. These and other similar laws effectively legislated the Chinese out of existence, giving rise to the saying that to have a "Chinaman's chance" was to have no chance at all.[10]

Throughout *Ah Sin* the Chinese character's very presence serves as a disruptive agent. The authors specify in the stage directions: "Ah Sin proceeds with his duties but is always in the way between the lovers at critical places" (54). Because his queue draws physical abuse, narrative actions must "pause" to allow for Ah Sin's entrance (78–79). In addition, all of Ah Sin's appearances on stage are brief. The character is almost always either displaced into a peripheral position by the narrative impetus or driven from the stage altogether. While he is central to the closing tableaux at the end of each act, all these exciting visual moments are displaced into the void between acts. Indeed, it could be said that the Chinese character seems to disappear at the very moment of his depiction. Still, Ah Sin is constituted as body, a presence, though admittedly one whose appearances are brief and disruptive.

The play also makes much of the impenetrability of the Chinaman, while York feels threatened by the laundryman's preoccupation with the "universal uncleanliness of the American people" and the Oriental countenance: "His face is as unintelligible as a tea chest" (29). The inability to understand the Chinese reduces the Ah Sin character to the generalized John Chinaman of Bret Harte's earlier writings: "The expression of the Chinese face in the aggregate is neither cheerful nor happy. . . . There is an abiding consciousness of degradation, a secret pain or self-humiliation, visible in the lines of the mouth and eye. . . . They seldom smile, and their laughter is of such an extraordinary and sardonic nature — so purely a mechanical spasm, quite independent of any mirthful attribute — that to this day I am doubtful whether I ever saw a Chinaman laugh."[11] Harte describes the typical Chinese face: "His complexion, which extended all over his head except where his long pig tail grew, was like a very nice piece of glazed brown paper-muslin. His eyes were black and bright, and his eyelids set at an angle of 15°; his nose straight and delicately formed, his mouth small, and his teeth white and clean."[12] Later, Harte claims that despite the surface cleanliness, the Chinese "always exhaled that singular medicated odor — half opium, half ginger — which we recognized as the common 'Chinese smell.' "[13]

With "mechanical spasms" for laughter, a "Chinese smell," eyes at a 15-degree angle, and "brown paper muslin skin," a generalized Chinese character such as Ah Sin becomes little more than an assemblage of fetishized fragments, comprising the most obvious aspects of difference. Accordingly, while provided with a presence on the stage, the Ah Sin character exists as an absence rendered through attributes that emphasize the Chinese character's marginality and foreignness. Visually, Ah Sin was constituted as an absent body within a loose-fitting shapeless tunic which served to neutralize any potential male threat. Wearing a conical hat, Ah Sin's hair was braided into a long queue to provide him with a "tail on top of his head instead of where it ought to be." In his essay entitled "John Chinaman," Harte describes the slippers worn beneath puffy pantaloons, both a standard part of the Chinese character's dress: "To look at a Chinese slipper, one might imagine it impossible to shape the original foot to anything less cumbrous and roomy."[14] In action, he always displayed the "monkey faculty of imitating" (52–53).

Not all of Ah Sin's actions were mere imitation. For an observer today, if not then, his actions or inaction employ a radically different strategy. Ah Sin is not a character defined by his constructive activities and role within the play; rather, he serves as an absence suspended in tension, defined not by his actions but by his obliquely constituted parts. Rather than providing action, Ah Sin serves as an agent subversive to consistent narrative action. And even at the end of the piece, when he produces the telling evidence, he ironically cannot testify himself but can only serve as bearer of the information, which in silence speaks more loudly than he can.

Although Ah Sin is devoid of a significant physical presence, the stage was filled by fetishized impressions of Chineseness, fragments which stand in for the Chinese, who had not yet appeared on America's East Coast. If the American audiences of the day had difficulty reading the face of the displaced/displacing Chinese character, the task was made even more confusing by the use of a white player in the role of Ah Sin. Still, like Mark Twain, major newspaper critics praised Parsloe's portrayal: "Mr. Parsloe's Chinaman could be scarcely excelled in truthfulness to nature and freedom from caricature." The critic of *The World* felt the performance flawed but good: "Mr. Parsloe's Ah Sin is a creation. He happily steers clear between delineation of the comicality of the character and the burlesquing of it. His make-up is good, except that he looks too pale for a Chinaman, and his ambling walk is a trifle exaggerated, but he avoids turning the stupidity of Ah Sin into the fun-making silliness of the low comedians."[15] It becomes clear that through Parsloe's portrayal of Ah Sin, the Chinese character was not only displaced but perhaps even erased from the map of American experience at the very moment of his depiction.

Although neither Mark Twain nor Bret Harte had bargained on such a subversively disfigured portrayal of Chineseness, their play was likely doomed the moment the decision was made to collaborate on a project geared to the mass theatre audience. Stepping out of their normal roles

MR. C. T. PARSLOE

AS

"AH SIN!"

as fiction writers, they failed to realize that the change in medium and audience would radically influence the way in which they could shape their characters. Jean Baudrillard, writing in the late twentieth century, identifies some of the problems:

> the plan is always to get some meaning across to keep the masses *within reason*; an imperative to produce meaning that takes the form of the constantly repeated imperative to moralise information: to better inform, to better socialise, to raise the cultural level of the masses, etc. Nonsense: the masses scandalously resist this. . . . they want spectacle . . . they idolise the play of signs and stereotypes, they idolise any content so long as it resolves itself into a spectacular sequence. What they reject is the 'dialectic' of meaning.[16]

Audience expectations ultimately determine all successful theatrical characters. And, it could be said that Mark Twain and Bret Harte's attempt at a sympathetic portrayal of the Chinese was subverted by this economic imperative.

Interestingly, monetary exchange—in the form of betting on dog fights and innumerable poker games[17]—is central to the play. Miss Plunkett speaks for others when she says: "This Californy's the land for me. I reckon there's no end of gold here, and fellows with loads of cash. Becky Simpson hadn't been in California a week til she married a hundred thousand dollars, with considerable of a man thrown in" (38–39). Indeed, monetary exchange provides a ground for Ah Sin's few assertive acts in the play. He overcomes his scruples against illegal activities when offered sufficient monetary return, and, finding illegal activity lucrative, he later considers criminal activities as a means of income beyond his "washee washee" business (41, 50, 68). By the play's end Ah Sin has accumulated over $11,000 and one-half interest in a gold mine, almost all achieved through shady dealings. The fetishization of money and its influence on the action of the play is a reflection of Twain and Harte's expressed purpose in writing the play—to make some money fast.[18] Their attempt, then, to exceed the conventions of the racial stereotype ultimately inscribes itself within the very conventions it sought to tran-

"His smile it was pensive and child-like."

From Ah Sin. *University of Wisconsin Libraries.*

"He went for that Heathen Chinee."

From Ah Sin. *University of Wisconsin Libraries.*

scend, leaving the Chinese character suspended but subject to the economics of mass entertainment.

The reviewer for *The World* aptly noted that "the language used [in *Ah Sin*] is distinctly American . . . and the incidents — the Heathen Chinese himself included — are American everyone."[19] Clearly, in America the only space in which the Chinese could comfortably reside was in the imaginary. As constituted within the American legal system of the nineteenth century, a good Chinaman came to be defined as one who made no impact whatsoever, or as Ah Sin announced, "Me not done nothing, me good Chinaman" (32–33). Mark Twain "pitied the friendless Mongol" and upon reflection offered a solution: "I wondered what was passing behind his sad face, and what distant scenes his vacant eye was dreaming of. . . . Money shall be raised — you shall go back to China — you shall see your friends again."[20] Indeed, finally aware of his position in the imaginary geography of the American West, the fictional Ah Sin character expresses his desire to absent himself, claiming that all he really wants is to "catchee plenty golde, mally Ilish girl, go back to China . . ." (11). This was precisely what many American politicians sought, to repatriate the Chinese — but of course keep their gold and the Irish women.

This rupture at the very site of representation, however, preserves an afterimage, a trace of the emergent image now voided of its contents, but maintained through power of the desire which engendered it. In creating a Chinese character for the theatre, Mark Twain and Bret Harte fell into a trap of their own making. Represented as absent and yet subject to the audience's desire to see the Chinese, Ah Sin exists within an ideologically enforced space of absence that invites political manipulation.[21]

4

Henry Grimm's
The Chinese Must Go
Theatricalizing Absence Desired

The grounds are so disposed as to disguise and to hide: something, always a body in some way. But also to disguise the act of hiding and to hide the disguise: the crypt hides as it holds. Carved out of nature, sometimes making use of probability or facts, these grounds are not natural.
— Jacques Derrida

Given the intensity of the political debate over the presence of the Chinese in America, the construction of the Chinese as Other was bound to occur in the social text as well as in theatrical productions such as *Ah Sin*. Shortly after Harte and Twain's play opened in New York, the California state senate formally submitted *An Address to the People of the United States Upon the Evils of Chinese Immigration* (13 August 1877). In this document the Chinese were declared:

morally, the most debased people on the face of the earth. Forms of vice, which in other countries are barely named, are in China so common that they excite no comment among the natives. They constitute the surface level, and below them are deeps and deeps of depravity so shocking and horrible that their character cannot even be hinted. . . . *Their touch is pollution*, and harsh as this opinion may seem, *justice to our own race demands that they should not be allowed to settle on our soil* (emphasis in original).[1]

Indeed, it was commonly held that "from seven-tenths to eight-tenths of the Chinese population of San Francisco belong to the criminal classes."[2] One must wonder how the Chinese could possibly pose a threat to the white labor market if seventy percent of the population was involved in criminal activity. Still, Chinese labor was blamed for every white social problem from hooliganism to venereal disease. Young men who could not find work because of the Chinese naturally became hoodlums for lack of gainful employment.[3] Accused of slave trading their women into prostitution rings, the Chinese were refigured to constitute a threat to the physical health of America:

> Their lewd women induce, by the cheapness of their offers, thousands of boys and young men to enter their dens, very many of whom are inoculated with venereal diseases of the worst type. Boys of eight and ten years of age have been found with this disease, and some of our physicians treat half a dozen cases daily. The fact that these diseases have their origins chiefly among the Chinese is well established.[4]

Indeed, not only were these women "designed for prostitutes" and "deprived of their womanly qualities," but the Chinamen themselves were "a nation of Sodomites, and . . . great numbers of boys and men like those shipped to this country were eunuchated when young."[5] These tracts exhibit not only a rationale for absenting the Chinese but also an early deployment of two stereotypes: the sexually available Asian woman and the sexually neutralized male. These figurations would stand in for the Chinese at the hoped-for vacant site of representation.

In addition, science was called upon to help justify the Sinophobia of the day. Some "advanced thinkers" of the period maintained "that competition is the truest test of superiority, and . . . that if American labor cannot compete with Chinese labor the fact proves its essential inferiority, and indicates the Chinese are the coming race."[6] An amusingly twisted social Darwinism emerged in response to Asian success: "The Chinese are very deceitful, and that very deceit is an indication of a weaker race. A weak man makes up in lying what he lacks in strength. They feel that weakness, and they conceal it by strategy and deceit."[7] Sinophobic ideology argued that despite their racial inferiority, Chinese

THE DIFFERENT NATIONS REPRESENTED IN THE COSMOPOLITAN CITY OF SAN FRANCISCO.

"Chinaman (Boss of San Francisco)." The Bancroft Library.

succeeded in the labor force not only because of their alleged deceitfulness but also because of an almost genetic "monkey faculty of imitating."[8] The Chinese "are quick at imitation. They learn by looking on. Then they go off in business for themselves. For businessmen to employ Chinese, is simply putting nails in their coffins. Every Chinaman employed will be a competitor. The result will be the driving from the country of white businessmen and white laborers."[9] Racist anti-Chinese magazine illustrations of the day articulate both the apparent relative success of the Chinese in San Francisco and the evolution of the Chinese from monkey to pig. Significantly, the illustrations employ the museum techniques of the list and survey to make their respective points. As was the case with museum displays, these graphic arrays of types no doubt proved persuasive to mass audiences. And finally, Reverend David Utter employed a medical analogy to make explicit his characterization of

Sinophobic Darwinism. The Bancroft Library.

the Chinese threat to not only California but the whole of America: "It is only a little cloud to-day, not bigger than a man's hand; but it has come to stay unless something is done, and will grow as a cancer grows till it poisons at last the whole system."[10]

Despite denials of wrongdoing from Chinese businesses, the Chinese — now constituted as depraved and deceitful — were locked into place by their once admired history: "their vices are bred in them by a civilization older than our ancient world, and there is nothing in human character on the face of this whole earth so stable, so fixed and sure and changeless, as the character of a Chinaman."[11] Science and history, notwithstanding, the Chinese also came under attack for their different family values: "The Chinese are bad for us because they do not assimilate and cannot assimilate with our people. They are a race that cannot mix with other races, *and we don't wish them to* [emphasis added]. The Chinese are bad for us because they come here without their families. Families are the center of all that is elevating in mankind, yet here we have a very large male population. And Chinese females that are here make this element more dangerous still."[12] Accordingly, it was decided that the "Chinaman is a factor hostile to the prosperity, the progress and the civilization of the American people."[13]

To a certain extent Ah Sin personified the position of the Chinese as a "factor hostile to" the narrative of American progress on the Western frontier. More important, however, was the emerging network of fetishized intertextual references which would define both the Chinese presence in concrete social terms and the perceived need to expel them. A centerfold cartoon entitled "The Chinese Invasion" from the 17 March 1880 number of *Puck* magazine provides an example. The San Francisco cry "The Chinese Must Go" is met by the New York plea "The Chinese Must Come — Help Wanted." And, protected by treaty obligations, the Chinese are depicted as rats fleeing the sinking ship of California and emerging on Manhattan Island. Other frames show the Chinese dominating a New York "Primary meeting of the Future" and displacing the Irish from New York trains: "Gittee out, you Ilish Heathen!" Finally, employing a visual pun for the "Chinese Wave," it becomes apparent that "The Chinese Make a Clean Sweep" of America. Thus deployed as

"The Chinese Invasion," from Puck, *1880. Library of Congress.*

characters in a fractured narrative cartoon, the Chinese — or, more to the point, the Chinese question — had become a national concern. Another *Puck* cartoon of 14 February 1886 makes explicit the response that much of Anglo-America felt appropriate to the Chinese presence.

Unlike the textually marginalized Ah Sin, who exists only as a disruption to the narrative line in Mark Twain and Bret Harte's play, Chinese characters are central participants in Henry Grimm's farce, *The Chinese Must Go* (1879). Present at both the beginning and end of the play, they provide a frame and are central to the action in virtually every scene in the play. *Ah Sin* offered up an example of the Chinese for cursory "study," with the implication that varied conclusions could be drawn. Grimm's intentions are more explicit:

How much money do you think those pigtails suck out of this State every year? . . . Five million dollars. . . . Now what would you think of a man who would allow a lot of parasites to suck every day a certain quantity of blood out of his body, when he well knows that his whole

"Hobson's Choice — You Can Go or Stay." Library of Congress.

constitution is endangered by this sucking process; mustn't he be either an idiot or intent on self-destruction? . . . Suppose those Chinese parasites should suck as much blood out of every State in the Union, destroying Uncle Sam's sinews and muscles, how many years do you think it would take to put him in his grave? [14]

Clearly, as with *Ah Sin*, the presence of Chinese characters does not signal any positive future for the Chinese in America. In this instance, the fetishized aspects of difference are animated to articulate white America's complaints against the race.

As the piece opens, two Chinese characters smoking opium pipes and speaking pidgin English confirm the worst fears of white America:

> white man big fools; eaty too muchee, drinky too muchee, and talkee too muchee. . . . By and by white man catchee no money; Chinaman catchee heap money; Chinaman workee cheap, plenty work; white man workee dear, no work — sabee? . . . Chinaman plenty work, plenty money, plenty to eat. White man no work, no money, die — sabee? . . . White man damn fools; keep wifee and children — cost plenty money; Chinaman no wife, no children, save plenty money. By and by, no more white workingman in California; all Chinaman — sabee? (1)

In the first dialogue with a white character, a Chinese man, Ah Coy, is seen demanding money for his services to the Blaine family, which has evidently grown dependent upon Asian labor for the day-to-day conduct of the household. Lizzie, the daughter of the house, regularly shares Ah Coy's opium pipe, while her brother Frank is a hoodlum. Their parents, Dora and William Blaine, constantly argue over who is to blame for the condition of the family: "The matter is that you are too damned fond of sitting in the parlor rocking yourself in the chair and reading trash instead of looking after your household affairs. There, I caught our girl smoking that nasty Chinaman's pipe. . . . why the devil don't you make her work?" After Dora accuses William of failing to find work for their son Frank, the attack on the Chinese continues: "Hav'nt [*sic*] I been hunting for a place for years? Isn't every factory and every store crammed with those cursed Chinamen?" (4). Setting aside Darwinism on the subject of Chinese competition, the Christian wife argues that "if the Chinese drive us out, it is His will, and we ought to submit to it" (15).

William Blaine makes explicit his perception of the Chinese impact on American family values: "My son is growing up in idleness, and idleness is the source of all mischief. As his father, it is my duty to impress the habit of working upon him; without it he cannot prosper. Work is the root of all lasting prosperity. Owing to the large immigration of coolies it is almost next to impossible to find any kind of work suitable for a boy of his age" (8). When the father finally locates a job for him as a boot-black, his son refuses it, preferring instead to continue in thievery. His assessment of the situation proven correct as far as his son is concerned, William Blaine continues his argument with his wife by attacking Chinese slavery: "man sells body and soul — turns actually a slave — only to satisfy the craving of his stomach. This very cause brings those hordes of Chinese to our shore; and if we allow the surplus millions of their country to invade ours, they will degrade us to the same level" (14). Grimm makes this suggestion of slavery concrete through the introduction of Slim Chunk Pin who also threatens Dora Blaine: "Madam, I am an agent of the powerful Six Companies, and I herewith order you to pay this Chinaman for his washing, and this Chinaman for his services; and mark you, if you don't, your life wont [*sic*] be safe for a minute" (5).

An important pivotal character, Slim Chunk Pin does not speak pidgin English, as do most of the other Chinese characters in the play. He makes one appearance, during which he threatens Dora Blaine, offers to broker the purchase of a business and a wife for one of the Chinamen, Sam Gin, and is rudely dismissed when he threatens the hoodlum son, Frank Blaine. Yet this is sufficient to establish him as the equivalent of a slave master who can interact with whites and control opportunities for his subjects.

Slim Chunk Pin, through the organization he represents, is the evil genius who not only animates the play but articulates California's Sinophobia. While Ah Sin's collocated aspects of difference marked him forever as other, Slim Chunk Pin's impressive ability to negotiate with the coolie and the decadent Westerner — two other constructed identities — creates a new order of representation. As a construction whose characteristics parallel those of the emerging industrial America, his importation and management of Chinese labor are central to the activities which threaten to reduce white labor to a status below that of machine.[15] A representative of "the powerful Six Companies," an organization accused of everything from slave trading to serving "the imperial designs of China," Slim Chunk Pin, then, is perhaps the most important figure in the play.[16] He makes clear Ah Coy's indentured slave status: "This is the sixth time in eight months we have furnished you with a situation, and now you are on our hands again. If we had all such chickens as you, the importation of coolies would be a bad speculation. You have not half paid your passage money yet." And, shortly thereafter, Slim Chunk Pin offers to sell to Sam Gin both a washhouse and "a nice looking China girl." For this transaction he produces a contract for the shipment of "two dozen choice girls, between the ages of twelve and fifteen" for verification (6). On the matter of China's alleged colonialist intentions, Slim Chunk Pin complains: "We can do without the white people altogether. Why should we allow them to always skim the cream from the milk; we have submitted to it long enough. In ten years more, California will be ours" (6). Yet, this character appears only briefly, just long enough to threaten Dora and be expelled by Frank. Virtually all of his activity takes place in what amounts to an overheard secret transaction in the transitional space between his two interactions with white characters, Dora and Frank Blaine.

Aside from the continual complaining about the Chinese, the white characters accomplish very little. The hoodlum son disguises himself as his sister to rob her lover and later abuses a minister who favors Chinese immigration. Throughout the play, often at seemingly the most inappropriate times, Frank repeats the phrase "The Chinese Must Go!" And, as in *Ah Sin*, physical abuse is heaped upon the Oriental characters. In one instance of such abuse, an Asian character complains to Lizzie, "Your brother damn hoodlum, he pullee my tail all the time." The sister offers the opinion that "they are all trying to pull you back to China" (4).

Finally, like the *Puck* cartoon strips, what one comes away with is a sort of museumlike survey of diorama scenes animating the Sinophobic fears of Anglo-America. Within this context the most significant deployment of a sinister Oriental character, Slim Chunk Pin, is allowed to operate only in the interstices between actions with whites, at the end of Act I. Interestingly, while this treatment seems not unlike Ah Sin's placement in Mark Twain and Bret Harte's play, some crucial differences exist. Ah Sin serves to obscure the presence of the Chinese because the character is conceived as a collocation of physical differences; he is an Anglo-American construction of a fetishized Mongolian racial representative. In Grimm's play, this same fetishized visual construction of Chineseness is deployed to animate white fears regarding Chinese labor.

Clearly, Grimm is not subtle in staging the attack on the Chinese of the popular imagination. The play seems especially awkward in its handling of the events which ultimately allow for closure. Easily the most important activity in the farce centers on the proposed sale of a "China girl" to Sam Gin, during which the sinister Slim Chunk Pin goes so far as to perform a reading of the contract to the audience. As noted earlier, this comes about in an encounter that lasts only long enough to reinscribe the fears of white America before the narrative continues.

The document which Slim Chunk Pin reads details the number, age, and price for each of the women contracted for delivery: "We feel happy to accommodate you with the required number, but are very sorry to charge you with ten dollars apiece more than the last lot we sent you; a good article is very scarce at present in the market, the producers in the country holding back their goods waiting for better prices, we will ship them by the next outgoing steamer, dressed as formerly in men's clothes, and hope that they may arrive in as good condition as they will leave this port" (6–7). Significantly, the women will dress as men during the time of their transport. With their gender thus neutralized, they will be able to pass through American immigration procedures disguised as Chinese men, who of course pose no sexual threat. According to the narrative, the ploy had been successful in the past, and many Chinese women had arrived in America through this deception.[17]

The disguise becomes a very telling device, for it not only validates the notion of the Chinese as an inferior race which can succeed only through deceit, it also allows the dreaded yet desired Asian woman to pass into America. From this pool of imported "China girls," who arrive in America desexed, androgynous, and nonthreatening, would emerge the construction of the sexually available Chinese woman, suitable for Anglo-American consumption, and thus representing the potential for the progeny of mixed blood who could truly "pass."

In Grimm's play both miscegenation and the expansion of the Chinese population in California are forestalled: the contracted-for China girl turns out to be only Frank Blaine in disguise, plotting to steal Sam Gin's money. All that remains at the close of the play is the figure of the neutralized Chinese male, bound and miserable as he babbles and recounts for the spectator how much money was stolen by Frank Blaine. Brute force (used to dismiss Slim Chunk Pin at the end of Act I) and deceit emerge as appropriate ways of dealing with the Chinese. Even Lizzie Blaine applauds the use of brute force in this context: "You caused the Chinese to be turned out of the house; that compelled me to work. Work cured my sleeplessness, and gave me an appetite. I am healthy like a fish . . ." (16). It becomes clear that the earlier Anglo construction of the deceitful Chinese was necessary as a justification for the tactics which white America would later deploy in their dealings with the Asians.

Deceit aside, one is also reminded of the importance of language: Slim Chunk Pin's most outstanding trait is his command of the English language, which allows him to interact with whites in a manner closed to less accomplished Chinese. Likewise, the Mandarin "priest" of Act IV speaks perfect English as a sign of his elevated educational level and ability to control the lower-class "coolie." Accordingly, as Frank schemes to steal Sam Gin's money, Blaine works with an Anglo-American accomplice who was "born and brought up in Hongkong by English parents; knows their [Chinese] customs and language" (17). With this deception, the Chinaman is at once denied a wife and his money, while any possible miscegenation and Asian progeny were refused a place on the American stage. The Chinese assault had been engaged and the enemy defeated, all without any Asian involvement, because of course the actors were white. The theatrical repudiation of Chinese characters mirrors the actual situation of the Chinese in the American West of the nineteenth century.

With Anglo-America cast as victim, the fear that commonly held expectations and prescribed borders — both sexual and labor-related — would be transgressed became the justification for containing the Chinese. Chinese who could "pass" became the most threatening and therefore the most appealing targets. The focus on illegal Asian female immigration and an amoral sexual economy heightened public outrage. These attitudes, articulated through the press, cartoons, and theatre, directly influenced the decisions in 1882 and 1892 to contain the threat by limiting Chinese immigration to the United States.

5 Panoptic Containment

The Performance of Anthropology at the Columbian Exposition

What is fascinating about prisons is that, for once, power doesn't hide or mask itself; it reveals itself as tyranny pursued into the tiniest details; it is cynical and at the same time pure and entirely "justified," because its practice can be totally formulated within the framework of morality. Its brutal tyranny consequently appears as the serene domination of Good over Evil, of order over disorder.
— Michel Foucault

By the last decade of the nineteenth century, America's "problem" questions of racial containment seemed to be settled. The native peoples had been conquered and were in full retreat with the cavalry in hot pursuit. The rapid disintegration of their culture created an absence which provided the site for the construction of the "American Indian." This mythology, which sought to assuage American guilt over its brutal treatment of the native peoples, arose under the banner of Christian progress, among various other explanations and rationalizations.[1] The Civil War seemed to provide an appropriate accommodation to the overt institutional enslavement of blacks, while the problem of Mexican immigration had yet to achieve full force. And, finally, the completion of the transcontinental railroad proclaimed America's dominion from coast to coast.

In many ways the most problematic racial issue had been the "Chinese Question." Comprising over ninety percent of the railroad's 10,000 workers, the Chinese were responsible for the completion of the western section of the transcontinental railroad. After the joining of the Central Pacific tracks with the Union Pacific Railroad at Promontory Point, Utah, in 1869, America could now follow its horizon of expectations from the Atlantic coast to the Pacific Ocean.[2] Ironically, this moment that the Chinese had labored to make possible also marks the beginning of the overt absenting of the Chinese. The famous photographs celebrating the drama of joining the West Coast to the East are significant for the fact that no Chinese are visible. While press accounts were more even-handed in their descriptions, the visual texts provided viewers with a panoptic reading devoid of Asian participation. While in some key industries the Chinese approached fifty percent of the labor force in California, they were not to be tolerated as participants in history. Over this railroad Americans from the eastern seaboard could observe the national dream of empire as the train progressed westward. The passengers' gaze bore witness to the disappearance of the buffalo, the Indian, and now the absenting of the Chinese.

But the train traveled in two directions, and the "political problem" which Mark Twain alluded to in his curtain speech for *Ah Sin* refused to disappear. Thus, in a broad sense, the insertion of the Chinese into the landscape of America was not unlike Ah Sin's involvement with the narrative of the play by Harte and Twain. Clearly, the Chinese represented an unwelcome intervention in the narrative of Anglo-America's conquest of the West. California's Chinese question soon became America's next racial containment problem, because the Chinese could now transport themselves to the East Coast over the railroad they had helped to build. Between 1870 and 1882 Chinese arrivals in the United States swelled from 10,869 to 39,579 per year.[3] With this steady annual increase, Chinese were settling in towns all over America. Everywhere they appeared, they proved to be a highly competitive labor force, so much so that many began to fear that Chinese labor might do to white America what white America had just done to the Indian. Could it be that in its thrust to the West Coast the superior Anglo-American Christian culture had just disposed of an inferior "Mongolian" native American race only

The Chinese absented from the Promontory Point celebrations. Library of Congress.

to be itself displaced by a newly arriving "Mongolian" horde from China? As Bret Harte put it: "Is our civilization a failure, Or is the Caucasian played out?"[4] Because they were willing to work for lower wages than their white counterparts, the Chinese became the defining element in the material conflict between the emerging labor organizations and management. Anti-Chinese sentiment in response to perceived threats to the Anglo-American standard of living arose in the form of race riots across America. Among the most notorious were those in Denver (1880), resulting in the displacement of over 400 Chinese from their homes and one death; in Rock Springs, Wyoming (1885), with twenty-eight dead Chinese miners; and in Snake River, Oregon (1887), with ten dead Chinese miners. In addition, many riots took place in California and Washington state. Hundreds of Chinese were driven from towns in Washington, where Chinese merchants were simply given one day's notice to pack up their goods and leave.[5] As the Chinese had been erased from the final moment of the Promontory Point visual text, so it would seem that the American public wanted them to disappear from the social text as well.

The demonization of the Chinese. California State Library.

Government in some rare moments of responsiveness acceded to the wishes of its citizenry. Beginning in the 1850s, California denied citizenship to "persons of Chinese or Mongoloid races," and later imposed a tax on the Chinese, with the funds going to "protect free white labor against competition with Chinese coolie labor." Still other laws in the 1870s were directed against "coolie slavery" and the importation of "Mongolian, Chinese, and Japanese females for criminal or demoralizing purposes."[6] All declared unconstitutional, these laws could not compare to the immediate impact of the 1882 Chinese Exclusion Act, America's first law barring the immigration of a targeted racial group. Chinese immigration had been contained. In 1883, the Chinese Exclusion Act, coupled with the clearly hostile Sinophobic environment in America, brought about a net loss of almost two thousand, while the year before (1882) had seen a gain of some 29,213 Chinese.[7] In 1893, after the Geary Act extended the 1882 legislation with severe deportation requirements, only 472 Chinese entered America, and these were likely of the wealthy, privileged class who can always find loopholes in exclusionary laws.

By 1893, the year of the Columbian Exposition in Chicago, the last apparent racial containment problem of the nineteenth century had been settled, and America looked to the future through the instrument of the Great White City, on the occasion of the four hundredth anniversary of Columbus's great "discovery." The Columbian Exposition of 1893 provides a unique opportunity to examine American racial representation at a moment when America could begin to articulate its dreams of empire.

The Chinese were nowhere to be found within the formal confines of the Columbian Exposition, although other races were represented in the department of anthropology and in the many pavilions devoted to foreign countries. The pavilions of the "Foreign Group" were small and situated in the northeast section of the fair, wedged in between the art galleries and large buildings relating to the United States government. While the political implications of the placement of the foreign pavilions seem clear, the department of anthropology found itself located in the extreme southeast corner of the site, below the exhibit of Krupp's Guns and surrounded by the leather, dairy, and livestock exhibits. On the grounds around the anthropology building, ethnographic exhibitions and reconstructions of Mayan ruins returned a culture long absent to visibility by means of a panoptic assemblage of objects. Artifacts from long vanished cultures stood in for history, geography, and racial difference.

While the smugness of imperialist desire is clearly articulated through the placement of these displays of racial representation, the manipulation and strategic absence of some racial groups demands closer consideration. While the likes of Japan, Guatemala, Ceylon, Siam, and India were represented within the confines of the official fair, neither the Chinese nor the African Americans were allowed a place. Mexico did not appear within a foreign pavilion but achieved visibility through recreated Mayan ruins on the grounds of the department of anthropology.

Representations of the native peoples of North America were perhaps the most interesting. An "Esquimau Village" represented the northern

reaches of Canada, but despite a whole winter "allowed to them for ac-
climatization," problems emerged: "No sooner did summer appear than
dissension arose; the fur coats were thrown aside, whereas the public
desired to see the customary habiliments of the North, and at last ten
of the twelve tribes set up a kingdom elsewhere, claiming that they
had been deceived by the contractor who had taken them from home."
Similar compounds were established for the "Quackuhl" and the Penobscot Indians of Maine.[8] Thus, as dominant-culture Americans wandered
about the dairy and livestock exhibitions, they could view living examples of these ethnic groups.

The Plains Indian tribes of the United States did not fare as well.
These Indians with whom the American cavalry had fought were represented in the department of anthropology as already-dead races.
While the Esquimaux colony forced into visibility living examples of
ethnicity, the Plains Indians could be found only as plaster mannikins
performing domestic activities in glass enclosed dioramas.[9]

The varying situations of the Mexican, the Chinese, the African
American, and the American Indian suggest different moments in the
process of representational containment. Obviously, those nationalities which did not constitute a threat were not obstructed. The African
American — with his unpleasant connection to the embarrassing institution of slavery — was missing. The Indian, who had just recently been
physically removed from the American field of vision, became visible
only as plaster representation, now reduced to an object, no different
from the glass jar containing Nebraskan corn. Mexico, disposed of
through war, but whose population stood poised to lurch into the American labor market like the Chinese, was excluded. Still, the ennobled
Indian could be revived in dioramas peopled by painted plaster characters which rehearsed the roles prescribed for them by their imperial masters. The Indian whose culture had been annihilated had escaped into
representation.

It seems that to qualify for enforced visibility, a racial representation
had to be not only historicized, but thoroughly constructed as alien and
contained. This was true of the Indian, but the Mexicans, blacks, and
Asians had not yet been completely textualized in this fashion. Of the

An ethnographic diorama of Plains Indians performing domestic tasks. State Historical Society of Wisconsin.

latter group, it seems the Mexicans were further along in the process because ruins validated their history. Blacks, numerous and broadly distributed in the midst of Anglo-American population centers, stood as a racial situation yet to be resolved. And the Chinese had only recently been awkwardly contained by the Chinese Exclusion Act of 1882 but were not yet controlled. Accordingly, it is not difficult to understand why the Chinese were not allowed a presence in the official survey of the new world order at the 1893 fair in Chicago.

Still, the acts of unofficial racial containment could not be stopped. There evolved during the planning stages of the Columbian Exposition a parallel, slightly less official, entrepreneurial adjunct to the sanctioned fair. Situated on land adjacent to the Columbian Exposition, this array of exhibitions charged admission fees to each of its many buildings. The official fair required only one admission fee to gain access to the grounds and all its exhibits. The adjunct fair came to be known as the Midway Plaisance and was the dominant stage for the articulation of racial containment at the 1893 event. Arrayed along a broad avenue extending for about a mile from the western edge of the official exposition, dozens of individual sites featuring examples of racial types from all the nations of the world were constructed.[10]

While the sanctioned fair employed the museum survey as the vehicle for strategic textualization of race in the service of an American imperial desire, the entrepreneurs of the Midway commodified this racial containment into a grand panoptic vision for consumption on a utopian stage. Walking west on the Midway Plaisance, the spectator strolled past Hagenbeck's Animal Show; a Javanese village; an Irish village; a Jahore village; a Turkish village with a Bedouin Arab show; a street in Cairo replete with temple, tomb, and conjurer; a Moorish palace; a Persian theatre; a model of St. Peter's; a Chinese village with theatre and joss house; Sitting Bull's log cabin; an "Arab Wild East Show"; and finally a military camp, presumably to maintain order and enforce racial containment. If spectators wearied of ground-level consumption, for a fee they could ride high into the air on the world's first large-scale ferris wheel (265 feet high) and avail themselves of a magnificent godlike view of the imaginary world constructed beneath. Shops and restaurants allowed fairgoers the chance to collect souvenirs as they might on an international tour, without having to travel beyond the south side of Chicago.

On display were the awkwardly constituted racial/national representations which would become the persistent images of the future. The ideology of imperialist desire became the guiding principle on the Midway. While the Columbian Exposition's department of anthropology reduced racial representation to bland displays of clothing, bones, work implements, or foods which stood in for the primitive absented cultures, the entrepreneurs of the Midway Plaisance featured living proof of racial difference with characters draped in facsimile artifacts inspired by the collecting of the department of anthropology. Hassan Ben Ali, traveling in Morocco, traded "phonographs, electrical toys, snapshot cameras and other things to tickle the barbarian fancy" and succeeded in gaining an audience with the Sultan of Morocco: "The Sultan gave the speculative Arabian permission to go to the remotest borders of his dominion and collect all the material he could find for the Moorish village he intends to establish at the Fair. . . . he has started for that portion of the Atlas mountains in the southeast of Morocco to find some dwarfs said to be there, and persuade them to accompany him to the western world."[11] And, once again, anthropology legitimized his search: a paper read before the British Association for the Advancement of Science identified the dwarves and labeled them the "Akka."

The presence and performance of these racial differences on the Midway gave the representations a persuasive quality which the inanimate artifacts of anthropology could never produce. Further, the Western ability to implement the act of will which brought to life these distant cultures seemed to affirm the correctness of the imperialist impulse which drove this enterprise. Indeed, in the flush of this acquisitive frenzy, federal legislation was passed allowing some Chinese special permission to enter the United States to participate in the Midway exhibitions.[12]

Within this context, the Chinese achieved a visual text in their first unofficial participation in an American world's fair.[13] Headed by a "Chinaman named Sling, who came from Ogden, Utah," the Wah Mee Exposition Company constructed the Chinese Building to include: "A Chinese Theatre, with regular performances by native artists, selected from the best companies in the Celestial Empire; a Joss House, with priests and attendants, revealing the methods of worship as practiced in China; a Tea Garden, giving a view of social life in the Flowery Kingdom, such as has never been seen before in this country; a Bazaar, for the sale of silks and curios; a Museum, with artistic wax figures and Chinese designs from human models, and relics of the time of Confucius. No visitor should fail to take advantage of this rare opportunity to study the customs, habits and products of this most interesting people."[14] The caption for a published photograph of the "Chinese Joss-House" attempted an explanation of Chinese religious beliefs:

The Chinese Building on the Midway Plaisance. State Historical Society of Wisconsin.

The Chinese are so little known to Americans that an attempt to describe their theology, iconography, or ecclesiasticism must nearly always descend to the ridiculous. It is, however, believed that, in the operation of their religion in American cities like New York and Chicago, the right to be priest or sexton is sold at auction each year at a sum of less than one thousand dollars. The sexton obtains a certain

The "Chinese Joss-House." State Historical Society of Wisconsin.

monopoly of joss candles, incense sticks, paper, oil, tea and punk. He also makes a weekly call at the laundries and stores of his people, collecting small joss-sums, usually twenty-five cents. In addition, when a worshipper changes his religion, the sexton gives him a personally conducted tour in the joss-house, for which perhaps a dollar is exacted. It is understood by Americans, at least, that the idols are often reviled and scourged, in cases where they have not obviously changed the luck of their devotees.[15]

This representation of the practice of religion in China articulates the Sinophobic fear of the economic threat which Chinese labor represented. Despite the author's claim that true understanding must descend to the ridiculous, he confirms his assertion by his treatment of the two men pictured in the photograph. Within a rather blockish Orientalist architectural confection designed by the firm of Wilson & Marble, two

Chinese men are seated. Which is the priest? Is the other a convert on his tour? Has he already paid his one dollar? The backdrop of a few selected Oriental objects with flowery wall treatments confirms connections with the "Flowery Kingdom," while the men in their long gowns certainly constitute no threat to American virility. What was Anglo-America to make of this religion, in which worship is transacted with the precision of commerce and a god who fails to perform is replaced? "In the bazaar, entrance to which was free, a very wise Chinaman, with huge and mirth-provoking spectacles, told fortunes to an admiring circle of men, women and children. The wise man had an interpreter, who read and explained the prophetic writings." Clearly, the wise man's free fortunes, like those in fortune cookies, celebrated the hoped-for accumulation of wealth on the part of the shopkeepers in the bazaar.

The desire to deny any possible positive relationship between the Chinese representations and business interests becomes clear in the description of the Chinese theatre: "A large troupe of actors played a drama called 'A God in Heaven,' with joss and other idols on the stage. Men impersonated female parts, as in the early days of our own drama. A perfectly hideous noise made on a great brazen gong rendered the stay of a Caucasian terrible in these precincts, and probably ruined the prospects of the enterprise."[16] The author clearly prefers to cast the Chinese not as an appealing, intriguing exotic worthy of "study" but as a disruption to a pleasant afternoon on the Midway. In addition, the reader is reminded that Chinese still used men to impersonate women, a primitive mode of production no longer used in the more sophisticated West.[17] To reinforce this, a pair of images display a "Chinese Female Impersonator" beside a "Chinese Beauty."[18] Although these photographs are typical of the thousands of photographs recording the "types" of people inhabiting the Midway, they reveal a great deal about how the Chinese were to be contained visually. Most of the published photographs of the other Midway racial types show their subjects actively involved in performance: Arabs on horseback in a "Wild East Show"; Egyptians conducting camel rides on the streets of an imaginary Cairo; Javanese offering a musical concert; Amazon warriors displaying their breasts; South Sea

The Chinese Theatre. State Historical Society of Wisconsin.

Islanders showing their huts. The two Chinese, however, while clearly constructed as foreign, appear devoid of background, as if a conscious decision had been made to leave them suspended in an unarticulated, yet contained, space. The scientific sensibility of anthropology serves to mark these characters as foreign. Significantly, at this moment in the process of becoming a commodity, the "Chinese Beauty" is shown from head to toe. Like a China doll, her form can be comprehended completely. The caption seems to question the appropriateness of her inclusion in the "World's Congress of Beauty":

> It is not known whether Mr. Knox and Mr. Hyde, the promoters of the Beauty Show, chose this lady, or engaged experts from the Flowery Kingdom to feast their eyes on the loveliness of Asia and select the fairest; but it is certain that the little person took small interest in the business, for she was often seen fast asleep in her chair, oblivious of the indifference with which the male generations of Caucasians passed her on their way to Fatma's Sultanic bower at the north end of the room.

"Chinese Beauty."
State Historical Society of Wisconsin.   *"Chinese Female Impersonator."*

Small and doll-like, she could be quickly dismissed as one hurries past to a more appealing dancer.

The caption for "Chinese Female Impersonator" offers the following insight:

> it still remains that the stage of China, like our own negro minstrel boards, retains the influences of a time when the histrionic art was in so low esteem that women were not allowed to take part as actors. The man photographed . . . impersonated a woman in the gong-pounding play of "God in Heaven," at the Midway Temple, and by shaking the flaps on his cap, and the imitation of the shrill Chinese female voice, drove sorrow away from its customary haunts in the laundries of South Clark street.

Unlike the two men in the Joss house photograph, whose floor-length gowns neutralize any potential sexual threat, this actor is textualized as a female impersonator and thus does not require a full-framed containment of his body, for he could not possibly constitute a threat. Indeed, even as an imaginary woman, his "shrill Chinese female voice" is welcome only in Chicago's Chinatown.

The pair of expressionless figures provides for the Western spectator an obvious site for the construction of meaningful difference. On the face of the "Chinese Beauty" the caption finds certainty that the "little person took small interest in the business" for which she was brought to America. Given the history of economic fear that earlier dominated portrayals of the Chinese, this would seem an amusing moment of constructed racial aporia. The Chinese Beauty sits doll-like, contained, unappealing, and incapable of competing with the attraction at the Sultanic bower. This Chinese woman is clearly not the threatening Asian whose importation and fertility could drive Californians to distraction. Likewise, the female impersonator, his gender confused, whose unpleasant performances are comprehensible only to his own people, appears impotent in the face of Sinophobia.

The Chinese threat had been contained. The representational apparatus had begun the initial steps necessary to transform a human presence into a completely constructed image. The aim, of course, was to keep the Chinese contained, in a constructed, foreign place. Already the requirements for marking the presence of this commodified Chineseness were beginning to emerge in an institutionalized framework. In both *Ah Sin* and Grimm's *The Chinese Must Go*, the Chinese constituted a disruption to the narrative of American progress. The newly surveyed and commodified Chinese characters had to be self-subverting, carrying within themselves an aporia of racial identity which rendered the representation exotically incomprehensible to the West while claiming a mysterious internal logic. This tension between a supposed internal logic and its inaccessibility to Anglo-American expectations gives rise to derisive humor. The surface requirements for this new figuration of Chineseness included neutralizing costumes of vaguely Oriental design and a background of artistically arranged exotic objects to suggest a foreign location.

Similar representational containment strategies had been deployed against the American Indian. The fetishization of aspects of difference that constituted the character of Ah Sin was evolving into a commodified figure capable of hardening into something not unlike the cigar-store Indian. Having achieved this level of racial determination, the Chinese had been prepared for museumlike containment beside the American Indian in glass-enclosed dioramic containment fields.

6

Animating the Chinese

Psychologizing the Details

When the number of Chinese in America could be counted on one hand, they were a novelty, an amusement worthy of a look and perhaps some cursory "study." As they became more numerous and a threat to dominant-culture labor, the Chinese came to be perceived as a disruption in the narrative of America's dream of empire. While legislative action denied entry into the country for those who sought to immigrate, the increasingly Sinophobic environment drove those who were already in the country into ghettos. In *Ah Sin, The Chinese Must Go*, and the staging of the Chinese at Chicago's Columbian Exposition of 1893, the methods deployed to achieve containment were diverse and energetic to the point of hysteria.[1] As is clear from the documentation of the Chinese participation in the Columbian Exposition of 1893, the visual construction of the Chinese consistently denied or at least disfigured the very real threat that the Chinese represented to white labor. While this representational containment was admittedly somewhat fanciful, it was clearly effective in a manner not unlike the inflammatory racist cartoons which were commonplace in the late nineteenth century. As the Geary Act extended the strictures of the 1882 Chinese Exclusion Act, America could begin to refine its methods of control. The primary task involved two operations: the neutralization of the Chinese within their containment fields and the establishment of newly constructed representations of Chineseness for American consumption.

Although their alleged sojourner status had been used as a justification for excluding the Chinese, many intended to stay in America despite the clear desire of the dominant culture to exclude them from the social text. Ironically, some Sinophobes found themselves arguing that the repatriation of Chinese would drain America of its wealth. The change in status necessitated the creation of new methods for the social and representational control of those who would remain in America. The displacement of their representations into merely exotic foreign sites no longer seemed sufficient.

While earlier representations in cartoons and photographs sought to absent the Chinese by displacing them into an imaginary Orient, many photographs from the turn of the century attempted to document populations confined in Chinatown. Indeed, these photographs established the optical phase of inscribing Orientals in America so persuasively that to this day, most Euro-Americans read Chinatown and Chineseness as the turn-of-the-century photographer did.

By 1885 the containment field for the Chinese in San Francisco consisted of approximately ten city blocks. A plat map of the period color-codes every property occupied by the Chinese so that the overall map of San Francisco appears as a white city in which Chinese-occupied cells stand out, like a cancer inhabiting the body of white America. Those Chinese who ventured outside this ghetto often risked their lives. Still, while clearly victims of an imposed geography, those residing within the ghetto were safe — so safe that children roamed freely, playing in the streets.

Inside these confines between 1895 and 1906, Arnold Genthe (1869–1942) produced over two hundred photographs documenting the Chinese "performance" of everyday life. Genthe was not a photographer who offered his images as social commentary; his pictures of

The Chinese contained. California State Library.

Chinatown were probably sold to wealthy patrons. Moreover, he conceived of his project in artistic terms, thereby containing and distancing the Chinese as fanciful aesthetic figures, frozen in time and arranged as objects — to be seen and comprehended as fetishes or souvenirs of a tour through the ghetto. After the great earthquake and fire of 1906, his photographs took on new significance as documents of an old San Francisco Chinatown now rendered an object of nostalgia by its total destruction. Indeed, in 1912, with the establishment of a Western-style government in the Republic of China marking the end of old dynastic rule and of the queue, Genthe's photographs more than ever seemed to persuade viewers that the Chinese as previously represented were on the verge of vanishing, or, worse still, in danger of assimilating. Not surprisingly, then, within a year or two of each of these defining moments in the representational history of the Chinese in America, volumes of Genthe's Chinatown photographs found publication. *Pictures of Old Chinatown* (1908) and *Old Chinatown* (1913) offer photographic and textualized extensions of the paternalistic tradition articulated earlier through the work of Bret Harte and Mark Twain. A more recent republication of his images, *Genthe's Photographs of San Francisco's Old Chinatown* (1984), with critical commentary by John Kuo Wei Tchen creates a rich intertextual field upon which new readings of Genthe's images can be achieved.

This contained imaginary terra incognito, not China and certainly not America, which persisted even after the earthquake and fire, could not be allowed to change, especially as the Chinese inhabitants might actually prove assimilable. Accordingly, control at this site of containment was absolutely essential. Genthe's photographs, combined with text by Will Irwin, provided a persuasive, if romantic, representation of what the Chinese and Chinatown ought to be:

> So the quarter grew into a thing like Canton and still strangely beautiful and unlike. Dirty — the Chinaman, clean as a whistle about his person, inventor of the daily bath, is still terribly careless about his surroundings. . . . But always beautiful — falling everywhere into pictures.
>
> . . . From every doorway flashed out a group, an arrangement, which suggested the Flemish masters. Consider that panel of a shop front in Fish Alley which is to me the height of Dr. Genthe's collection. It is a Rembrandt. Such pictures glimpsed about every corner. You lifted your eyes. Perfectly conceived in coloring and line, you saw a balcony, a woman in softly gaudy robes, a window whose blackness suggested mystery.[2]

While this suggested mystery became the "sign" for all things Chinese, the passage is most useful in detailing the textualization essential to the creation of the space into which Chineseness could be inscribed. The textual geography created had to be like, yet unlike, China (Canton); dirty, yet clean as a whistle; terribly careless, but always beautiful; pedestrian (from every doorstep), but perfect in line and color; and finally, a mystery. As a touristic geography, its consistency through time is astonishing. *The Pacific Tourist* had noted earlier that "the Chinamen seem to thrive best, and huddle closest where it is darkest and most dismal." Later, this same tourist guidebook comments: "Notwithstanding their foul habitations, they seem to come out of their filth as the eel from his skin, with a personal cleanliness that is marvelous, and to most incredible."[3] Like the descriptions of the "Chinese Female Impersonator" and the "Chinese Beauty" on the Midway Plaisance, the oppositions in this text displace Chinese subjects into the imaginary, beyond the realm of American experience.

The photographs — developed, fixed, neutralized, and, finally, cleaned before mounting and sale — provided Genthe's patrons with the necessary space of pristine mystery through which to explore Chinatown. These Chinese aliens, whose textual construction offered them up as radically disfigured beings, clearly could not occupy a space with recognizable landmarks. It is evident from the early publication of Genthe's photographs that he had no intention of disappointing his patrons: "The wealthy could now own an original print of an 'authentic,' irretrievable past."[4] The control and manipulation of the representations emanating from his Chinatown site became central to his project. Significantly, Genthe himself attributes his initial interest in Chinatown to a tourist guidebook:

> Like all good tourists I had a Baedeker. A sentence saying, "It is not advisable to visit the Chinese quarter unless one is accompanied by a guide," intrigued me. There is a vagabond streak in me which balks at caution. As soon as I could make myself free, I was on my way to Chinatown, where I would go again and again, for it was this bit of the Orient set down in the heart of a Western metropolis that was to swing my destiny into new and unforeseen channels.[5]

Genthe discovered, however, that the photographic representations of the absented Chinese, now forced back into visibility in a constructed foreign — yet not foreign — American environment, proved a difficult project. Like Edward Curtis's documentation of the vanishing race, the North American Indian, the subject and its containment field did not always cooperate.[6] Such was the case with Genthe's photographs of Chinatown. To capture photographically the kind of Chinatown Irwin describes was not an easy task. Accordingly, the intertextual spaces created by tensions between the photographs and the surrounding com-

"The 'Devil's Kitchen' By Night." Outline reveals Genthe's cropping of full-frame negative. Collection of John Kuo Wei Tchen.

mentary became the site for the construction of this next phase of Chineseness.

The caption informs the reader that the photograph represents " 'The Devil's Kitchen' By Night" and continues: "All who have followed a guide through Chinatown will remember this show-place. The quarters which tourists paid to 'see the hop fiends' kept it going for years."[7] A reminiscing tourist recalls the performance of a "hop fiend":

> he looked incredibly ancient. His face was like wrinkled parchment, his body a mere dried husk that gave no contours to his sagging clothes. He was toothless, as may be imagined and he possessed two things — a faithful cat, and a mysterious slab of onyx set in an ebony frame supposed to exert a charm on all who left money for the purpose. His mind was clear enough to promote the sale of these charms and once this matter was settled, he would stretch out in his bunk and treat his visitors to an exhibition of opium smoking.[8]

As early as 1885, a tourist manual suggested employing off-duty police officers as guides for tours through this part of town. Tchen's research reveals that the "Devil's Kitchen" photograph depicts a site behind Jackson Street where three tenement buildings enclosed a courtyard: "Hundreds of elderly and unemployed men lived in this quarter. The courtyard itself served as a common space equipped with a public kitchen housed in a wooden shed. These were among the poorest residents of Chinatown. In order to survive they banded together, sharing what they had, living and eating cooperatively."[9] Were all Chinese communal kitchens the "Devil's Kitchen?" Or, had the poor of the commune found an easy way to separate a tourist from his money by merely performing to comply with white expectations? And, one must wonder whether the man depicted was merely a resident of the commune or a "hop fiend," as the early twentieth-century observer assumed.

Of course, the emphasis on filth in both Irwin and earlier guidebook writers was necessary to match the other half of the dyad, the equally constructed clean and desirable aspect of Chineseness. Throughout the volume, Genthe and Irwin go about reinscribing the fetishes of the century before: Chinese slave trade, tong murders, curious religious practices, Chinese theatre with its incomprehensible music, gambling, the elaborate tunnels beneath Chinatown, odd occupations. However, this work necessarily exceeded the mere containment efforts of the previous century, because the Asian alien now resided within the body of white America, and, despite the clearly hostile environment, he showed no sign of leaving or disappearing anytime soon.

The image of the "Toy Vendor" is at first glance an innocuous photograph perfectly described by its caption.[10] No subcaption was deemed necessary, for the requisite exotification had been performed internally. This photograph had been published earlier in 1899 with the title "Chinese New Year." The pre-earthquake publication of this photograph showed a background which included a sign in English and seemed to offer Chinatown as a community in which whites and Chinese freely interacted. Between 1899 and 1908, as the Chinese community demonstrated its ability to persevere even in the face of concerted governmental attempts to relocate the community after the fire, attitudes toward the Chinese changed. Tchen describes Genthe's adjustments: "The elderly man in front is selling Chinese dolls sitting in rickshaw carts. In an effort to make the background concession stand appear more exotic and foreign, Genthe etched out the English words 'Chinese/Candies/5 Cts./Per Bag' and published this photo . . . with Chinese words written in."[11] Evidently, the level of commercial exchange between the Chinese and Anglo-America now seemed undesirable to the authors. The Chinese had to be reconstituted as forever foreign, despite their presence in America.

Before descending to the reinscription of earlier Chinese stereotypes, now refigured and contained in Chinatown, the Irwin text rehearses the "noble savage" motif once enforced upon the American Indian: "They were an honest people — honest beyond our strictest ideas. . . . Our pioneers cut off their sacred pig-tails, cast them forth disgraced, beat them, lynched them. . . . [They viewed] this heroic people, possessed of a passive fortitude beside which our stoicism is cowardice, as poltroons. With a dignity all their own, they suffered and went about their business, though death lay at the end."[12] The noble savage reconfigured begins the necessary psychologizing of Chineseness.

"Toy Vendor." The outline reveals Genthe's cropping of full-frame negative. Note the etched out sign into which Genthe later inserts Chinese characters. Collection of John Kuo Wei Tchen.

Unlike the placeless anthropologically correct "foreign" Chinese photographs of the Midway Plaisance, the representation of the toy vendor was allowed a place in America, but only if the site was constructed as foreign despite its American locale. Using a series of contrasts, Irwin guarantees against any possible assimilation: "Out of his mental difference from us, his oblique thinking as contrasted with our straight reasoning, his subtlety as contrasted with our directness, his commercial honesty as contrasted with our comparative commercial dishonor, his gentility as contrasted with our rudeness; further, out of our wholly unnecessary persecution and race hatred, he has come to a superior contempt of us and our ways."[13] Irwin goes on to note that "in the main, they feel a passive contempt." Still, when the apparently contained Chinese get drunk, they sometimes reveal themselves to be the hateful beasts they really are:

> as they drank and played . . . something deep below the surface came out in them. Their shouts became squalls; lips drew back from teeth, beady little eyes blazed; their very cheek bones seemed to rise higher on their faces. I thought as I watched of wars of the past; these were not refined Cantonese, with a surface gentility and grace in life greater than anything our masses know; they were those old yellow people with whom our fathers fought before the Caucusus was set as a boundary between the dark race and the light; the hordes of Genghis Khan; the looters of Atilla [sic].[14]

Thus psychologized, the alien Chinaman's apparently amiable efforts to adjust to American life could be dismissed as a mask for hidden, unarticulated nefarious intentions. The author notes that even the most apparently docile houseboy maintained a secret life on his day off which likely included gambling, opium, and other unspecified debaucheries.[15] Rendered forever untrustworthy, the Chinese could not be allowed to lead normal existences, for the threat had to be maintained. Even street life was refigured to constitute an exotic threat from within.

Worthy of note are the children in the "Toy Vendor" photograph. Tchen explains that easily one half of all the Genthe photographs prominently feature children. Many of these were the American-born children

"No Likee!" Outlines reveal Genthe's cropping for both published photograph and small exhibition print. Collection of John Kuo Wei Tchen.

of the feared yellow horde. Although in the Western context white children would normally be read as a promise of a bright future, the Chinese youngsters in the published volume of photographs occupy an ambiguous space at best.

Genthe's photograph "No Likee!" includes a subcaption: "The children imitated their elders; the big brother or sister, caring for little Ah Wu or tiny Miss Peach Blossom of the lily feet, scattered fearfully from the foreign touch."[16] This subcaption is excerpted from a section of Irwin's text detailing the condescending manner which the Chinese allegedly employed in their dealings with white America. The segment of text appears on the verso page opposite the photograph. Somewhat overdetermined by this subcaption, the image of a pair of children scrambling across a street no doubt imparted awkwardly ominous feelings of what the future might hold as these youngsters grow up to be just like their untrusting elders. Beyond this, the technique which Genthe uses to bring about this photographic moment is revealing.

Tchen's publication of the full-frame print of the original negative shows a much larger scene with little to indicate that the children are fleeing anything. The small child's hand is upraised to allow it to maintain balance while attempting to negotiate a proportionally high sidewalk curb. In fact, with some eighteen or nineteen individuals looking and walking off in various directions, there is little in the image to suggest anything other than an almost random moment of Chinatown street life, one of the many images which Genthe made of the backsides of Chinese to feature their queues. If the image of the children with their long queues was published to highlight this visually prominent aspect of racial difference, and the written intertext employed to make explicit the future immutability of this difference, then still another corner of this larger image underscores a more sinister agenda.

In the upper right-hand corner of Tchen's full-frame print there stands a solitary figure wearing dark slacks, a light coat, and a Western-style hat. Within the context of the almost random moment captured within this large frame, the character is just another figure staring off into the distance up Washington Street. Be that as it may, Genthe apparently found this man's pose worthy of closer study. In the Library of Congress, there exists a small exhibition print by Genthe in which this figure stands alone, with all else cropped out of the image. Somehow, with his right hand jammed into his pant pocket and his left hand resting on his right shoulder, this man wearing a Western-style hat captured Genthe's attention. But why set him off in isolation from his environment? And why did this Westernized Chinaman not warrant inclusion in the collection of photographs of Chinatown? Perhaps his image destabilized or threatened the fundamental assumptions that justified the whole project. Ambiguities and complexities of this nature were to be denied.

Ambiguous and sinister qualities operate most effectively in those moments when "blackness suggested mystery." And even in the brightness of the larger negative of the "No Likee!" image, Genthe could create the threatening Chinese of the future. He carefully controls the contrast of light to dark and crops to exclude the light-colored upper story of the building across the street, while leaving the street litter to serve as foreground to the children negotiating the curb.

Likewise, to create a dark sensibility in his photograph "New Year's Day Before the Theatre," Genthe carefully crops to exclude light elements.[17] The published piece shows a small crowd apparently waiting for the doors of the theatre to open. It is clearly a festive event. A gayly attired woman and child appear in a crowd of men whose queues are once again captured on display for the white observer. Most intriguing are the aspects removed from the image in the 1908 published version. In Tchen's published full-frame print, Genthe himself makes an appearance in the lower right corner. In the full-frame version, it is likely that he went through some effort to insert himself into the image; indeed, Genthe seems the only person aware of the camera's presence. Still, it is not entirely clear why Genthe, after situating himself in the photograph, removed himself from the published print. That he crops himself out appears consistent, however, with a desire to show Chinatown as a totally Chinese enclave, a site beyond the likely experience of Anglo-America. This process of selection is typical of the visual control Genthe exercised over the gaze in his first published volume of Chinatown photographs. He felt it necessary, even to the extent of excising himself from the Chinatown he clearly enjoyed photographing, to maintain the locale as a discrete entity which could neither contaminate nor be contaminated by white America.

In 1900, Ira Condit complained that the Chinese were becoming too American: "Chinatown swarms with children. As one goes along the street, they are seen at every turn and in every nook and corner, playing very much after the fashion of American children. Indeed it is often painful to see how Americanized they are becoming."[18] The photo-texts by Genthe and Irwin inscribed the performance of Chinese America as never assimilable, always alien to contemporary American life. With the Chinese thus contained in Chinatown and their representations controlled, Irwin could proclaim the transformation of the Chinese in America "from our race adversaries to our dear, subject people."[19]

"New Year's Day Before the Theatre." Collection of John Kuo Wei Tchen.

In 1913 Genthe finally allowed himself a presence in Chinatown. In his published photograph "An Unsuspecting Victim," Genthe, holding his camera, stands before a Chinatown building. An elderly Chinese man with a quizzical expression on his face gazes at Genthe, who seems preoccupied with his small camera. In the lower right corner of the image stands a young Chinese child in holiday dress. Tchen's full-frame print reveals how Genthe achieved the published print. In order to inscribe himself into a purely Chinese environment, Genthe cropped out a figure

"An Unsuspecting Victim." Unretouched image from original negative is at right.
Collection of John Kuo Wei Tchen.

on the right side of the negative. This figure, a young man dressed in Western attire, was likely deemed too acculturated for the old Chinatown of the book title. More impressively, Genthe also obliterated a bearded white man standing beside him. The old Chinatown of the imaginary, now proving uncooperative, had to be reconstructed. While the published print with Genthe in place would appear to run counter to his desire to construct Chinatown as a purely Chinese ghetto, it in a sense strengthens the Anglo-American claim to visual control. For his presence in an otherwise purely Asian visual field both validates his authority as the maker of images of the Chinese in America and also authenticates his constructed images. Like the only anthropologist to visit a "primitive" culture, Genthe alone — by virtue of his many years of photographing Chinatown — could claim authority to document, analyze, and disseminate. Indeed, he suggests that he alone dared go unaccompanied into this place of mystery: "Only once in my ramblings was I in danger. An English photographer whom I had met said he would like to take some night pictures of the 'Devil's Kitchen.' Had I been alone I would have had no fear, but going there in this instance involved a responsibility, and I asked the Chief to detail a detective to accompany us."[20] So, in "An Unsuspecting Victim" Genthe stands alone, between the untrustworthy elderly Chinese man "with parchment like skin" and the young child whose future will reinscribe the past of his elders. The present generation of Chinese is not so much "present" in its own identity — or range of complex identities — but "re-presented" as aestheticized figures in a mythic construct, while psychologized past and future generations are reinscribed as forever foreign, unassimilable. Thus subjugated and commodified in anthropologically correct images, these constructed Chinese were ready for the early cinema to animate their performance of their everyday lives.

Like Genthe's still photographs, the early moving pictures focused on aspects of difference. *A Chinese Shaving Scene* (1902), only thirty-five seconds long, features the shaving of an essentially bald scalp for the maintenance of the queue. *A Scene in a Chinese Restaurant* (1903), twelve seconds long, demonstrates the use of chopsticks. In *Scene in Chinatown*

(1903), twenty-two seconds long, a street scene shows whites wearing suits and the Chinese in their simple dark pajamalike clothing.

Brief constructed narratives also appear. *Chinese Laundry* (1894), twenty seconds long, offers a comic chase scene through two doors. *Chinese Rubbernecks* (1903) briefly reworks a vaudeville act in which one Chinaman catches another by the head. As the former attempts to pull his captive back into camera view, the neck stretches to reach halfway across the room. When the head is released it snaps back. Interestingly, one of the more ambitious of these early narratives clearly intended to reinscribe much of the sense of the Irwin text. *The Heathen Chinese and the Sunday School Teachers* (1904), while only one minute and forty-four seconds long, places before the spectator an apparently well-intentioned racial exchange run amok. Several Sunday-school teachers visit a Chinese hand laundry to deposit and pick up their wash. In the process they invite the heathen workers to attend Sunday school. After the visit to the Sunday school, the Chinese return the favor by inviting the women back to the laundry. They enter a back room of the laundry to find an opium den. The Sunday-school teachers along with the Chinese men smoke opium pipes together, and all seem to be having a good time until the police raid the laundry and arrest the men. This brief film closes with the Chinese men locked up in jail, while the women visit to present flowers. Appropriately, all the Asian roles are performed by white men, for who could know better how to demonstrate Euro-American expectations of Chineseness?

While *The Heathen Chinese and the Sunday School Teachers* appears light and airy, it clearly inscribes the notion of the hardworking Chinese whose secret daily life remains outside of the bounds of normal Anglo-American behavior. And, like most of the isolated brief cinematic representations of the period, these Chinese were consistently portrayed as fetishes consisting of collocated aspects of difference, forever foreign. By the beginning of the twentieth century, with staged newsreel events standing in for events in China, Chineseness had achieved the desired level of malleability.[21]

7 Casualties of War

The Death of Asia

on the American

Field of Representation

The Vietnam War. A group of soldiers on patrol capture a young and attractive Vietnamese woman. She is forced to accompany them on patrol and to satisfy their sexual wishes. As the soldiers begin to fear discovery of their highly illegal hostage-taking practice, they kill her. *Casualties of War* (1989), the recent star vehicle for Michael J. Fox, recounts the story. In her treatment of the "undoing of women," Catherine Clement asserts that only through her death does the character Cho-Cho-San in *Madama Butterfly* emerge as a true Asian character: "Butterfly, whose Japanese name is masked in Italian by the English signifier for an insect, regains her country at the same time she dies a Japanese death."[1] While this is merely a passing comment in Clement's impressionistic feminist reading of opera, it provides the outline for a larger trajectory relating to the troubling new tendency for Asians (both female and male) to find death on the American field of representation.

Generally speaking, performances displaying Asianness before the end of the nineteenth century were part of an imperialist institution of representation which seemed to be preoccupied with containment and control of the Chinese in particular and Asians in general. The tendency to show the Asian as witless, sexless, and therefore harmless emerged as the Western colonialist powers were consolidating their economic subjugation of East Asia. This forced "opening" of Asia required that the victors return with trophies of their greatness. As the ancient Romans articulated their imperial power through the display of foreign slaves and curious animals, so the nineteenth-century apparatus of representation produced harmless human entities for educational display and anthropological amusement. Asians, of course, were just one of many stereotypical ethnic creations peopling nineteenth-century stages. Unlike the Europeans, whose initial stereotypical stage representations would ultimately be replaced by dominant title-role characters in realistic dramas, Asians in America were denied access into the realm of the real.

Still, while the images were unflatteringly disfigured, reflecting the Sinophobic environment of the time, they at least grudgingly allowed the Chinese a presence on the American stage. As the Chinese representations were psychologized, and thus naturalized, the troubling new tendency emerges, that of the dead or dying Asian. It may be significant to note that at about this time one of the newly "opened" and supposedly subjugated East Asian powers was beginning to behave in a fashion not unlike its European mentors. Japan early on understood the need to confront the West in a European manner. In colonizing pieces of Korea, China, and other parts of East Asia, its agenda began to resemble that of the Western powers. To the extent that it defeated Russia in the Russo-Japan War of 1904–1905, Japan clearly constituted a threat to the Eurocentric perception of the new world order. As is all too often the case, the Western response was simply to eliminate the threat. The newly constructed "yellow peril" scare did not distinguish among Asian ethnicities — all of Asia collapsed into one yellow horde in the American imagination. In representational terms this meant the previously non-threatening, laughable portrayals of Asianness would be transformed into figures worthy of death.

Inspired by the success of John Luther Long's *Madame Butterfly* (1898) in short story form, New York playwright/director David Belasco collaborated with Long in 1900 to produce the mythic stage representation of *Madame Butterfly*. While these early projects enjoyed some success, it was not until Puccini's operatic rendering of *Madama Butterfly* (1904) that the killing of Asia on stage achieved truly international dimensions. Both the John Luther Long narrative and the Puccini opera achieved early cinematic inscriptions. *Madame Butterfly*, as a narrative film starring Mary Pickford, appeared in 1915, while the film opera with Sylvia Sidney singing Cho-Cho-San came out in 1932. And of course many more versions would follow.

The story of *Madame Butterfly* is well known. Pinkerton, a bored U.S. naval officer stationed in Nagasaki, fakes a wedding to develop a liaison with a local Japanese woman. After he departs, she gives birth to his child and then anxiously awaits his return. Pinkerton returns, of course, with his elegant American wife, but only to claim his child. Because "death with honor is better than life with dishonor," the only action left open to Cho-Cho-San is suicide.

In *Madame Butterfly*, then, the Asian ceased to be a novelty from which the West could learn or at least find amusement. Asia ceased to exist as a place whose ancient wisdom might provide secrets to help America. Rather, Asianness was reconstituted as an object to be looked at, still, but now pinned to a board with a precisely placed needle through its heart. Although increased contact between Asia and America offered an opportunity for real understanding and exchange, American dramatists, with the characteristic provincialism of the Eurocentric colonialist way of looking at the world, began killing off Asians — as if to articulate an unwillingness, an impatience, or simply a lack of desire to understand.

Once the collocated aspects of difference hardened into stereotypes on the stage of America's East Coast, the apparatus of the newly emerging representational cinema fixed it permanently, enshrined it, inscribed, and inserted it into the popular text of American consciousness. One of the first feature-length films to exploit the suicidal neutralized Asian male was D. W. Griffith's *Broken Blossoms* (original title, *The Chink and the Child*, 1919). The film features Lillian Gish as Lucy, the daughter of

Madame Butterfly. *Wisconsin Center for Film and Theatre Research, State Historical Society of Wisconsin.*

a murderously brutal prizefighter. After a vicious beating administered by her father, Lucy collapses before the "Chink" storekeeper, whose subsequent developing love for the girl can only end in tragedy. Characterized as dreamy, frail, and sensitive, the "Yellow Man" can offer only a love devoid of sexuality. A love so pure, so exquisitely sacred, and ultimately so tediously maudlin that only suicide seems to provide proper closure. Indeed, the elements of the film fit together so well that any other ending would be unacceptable: death is this "yellow man" 's destiny. Intended as a sympathetic treatment of the Asian character, the film displays the latent anti-Asian racism inherent even in "liberal" representational projects of the time.

The subsequent popular cinema is full of such figures. The list of suicidal Asian emperors, princesses, and soldiers seems endless, while

Broken Blossoms. *Wisconsin Center for Film and Theatre Research, State Historical Society of Wisconsin.*

whole careers in the industry centered on characters whose final act involved death, preferably by their own hands. American-born Chinese actress Anna May Wong (1907–1961), whose film life featured many such scenes, once commented: "When I die, my epitaph should be she died a thousand deaths. That was the story of my film career. Most of the time I played in mystery and intrigue stories. They didn't know what to do with me at the end, so they killed me off."[2] Fittingly, in her obituary it was indeed noted that "as an Oriental temptress in exotic thrillers, the sloe-eyed beauty invariably wound up shot, knifed or poisoned." Another commentator summarized her roles: "She was the double-crossing Mata Hari who met her just deserts, the siren caught up in the insidious plans of Fu Manchu, the vamp who seduced the youthful American as part of an Oriental plot."[3] Clearly, not only did Wong's career typify the dying Asian motif, she participated in the initial feature-length cinematic inscription of most of what we associate with Asian femaleness.

Achieving fame through her performances in *Shanghai Express* (1932), in which she acted opposite Marlene Dietrich, and *Daughter of the Dragon* (1931), Anna May Wong had established herself earlier as Asian America's first significant silent-film actress. Her work in the silent film *Old San Francisco* (1927) is perhaps most typical, for in this relatively early feature piece can be seen not only the American cinema's emerging stereotypes but also the psychologizing strategies deployed to justify them.

Old San Francisco, like Genthe's photographs of old Chinatown, attempts to reconstruct a nostalgic, honorable, bygone era of San Francisco — in this case, a time before the city was corrupted by the crassly commercial interests which came to dominate San Francisco after the gold discoveries of the mid-nineteenth century. An early intertitle reveals the real focus of the piece: "The Chinese question had long vexed San Francisco. To keep the Mongol within the limits of Chinatown. . . . What graft and cruelty were invoked." It turns out, however, that Chris Buckwell, the chief "persecutor of the Chinese," proves equally dastardly in his treatment of the Vasquez family, who represent the landed gentry of a more refined earlier era. He viciously pursues a scheme to contain the Chinese in their ghetto while trying to evict the old landed gentry from their rancho on the outskirts of town. His irrational drive to achieve wealth and acquire property initially appears as simply part of the material drive of the late nineteenth century. After he terrorizes the patriarch of the Vasquez family to death, Dolores Vasquez, now the last of her line, is reduced to praying to God for vengeance. Her prayer is answered as the reason for Buckwell's evil behavior becomes clear: "In the awful light of an outraged, wrathful Christian God, the heathen soul of the Mongol stood revealed." Dolores Vasquez continues: "In a flash that hideous Buckwell revealed himself — and in his soul he knew that I knew — he is a Mongolian!" Accordingly, the whites, now cast as victims in their own land, decide to "submit Buckwell to the law and punishment of his own people." During the course of the film, as Buck-

Old San Francisco. *Wisconsin Center for Film and Theatre Research, State Historical Society of Wisconsin.*

well visits the "Chinese shrine and the god he worships," the spectator is introduced to Buckwell's brother, a dwarf whom Buckwell keeps in a cage. Both Buckwell and his dwarf brother stand as products of miscegenation, one demonically irrational in his pursuit of wealth and the other physically deformed. As psychologized in the film, Buckwell lives in a world of self-hate, seeking revenge on both the Asian community and the white for the mixing of the races that resulted in both his deformed nature and his dwarf brother's physical condition. Once again only his death can bring about proper closure.

Loyalty to her race requires complicity on the part of the Chinese girl played by Anna May Wong. Just as Buckwell appears trapped by the justice of both communities, the Anna May Wong character frees the evil Chinaman for the obligatory chase scene through "the labyrinths of that mysterious 'Inner Circle' — as remote from occidental life as the alleys of Tientsin or the gorges of the Yangtsze." Dolores Vasquez, now under Buckwell's control, is about to be sold into slavery. Her situation hopeless, she once again prays. This time her prayer is answered by the onset of the San Francisco earthquake of 1906, which devastates the city while crushing the life from the evil Buckwell. The heroine survives. The film ends as the dwarf climbs out of the rubble to dance on the dead body of the evil Buckwell, his brother. Both the Anna May Wong character and the Asian villain who could "pass" as a white man are dead, leaving behind the clearly disfigured dwarf as a visual reminder of the dangers of miscegenation. Again, the Chinese are contained in Chinatown and their representations at once animated and controlled, in this case under the threat of genetic disaster.

While the death by natural catastrophe of the Asian villain Buckwell follows the expected formula, the off-screen death of the nameless Chinese girl played by Anna May Wong has a deeper significance. In *Old San Francisco*, this female accomplice appears sexually available to Buckwell, despite his clearly evil intentions. And, in one scene they seem to come within inches of kissing, which is remarkable because motion picture rules of the time forbad the portrayal of such acts between representatives of different races. Spectators understood that Warner Oland, the actor who played Buckwell, was white, despite his representing a Chinese character. Still, the cinematic inscription of Asian female promiscuity naturalizes the nineteenth-century Anglo-American construction of Chinese women. The position of the Chinese in the nineteenth century precluded the presence of women. The men exploited for their labor were not allowed to have families. Because Chinese men were constituted in the popular consciousness as sojourners who only desired to return to China after accumulating wealth in America, the presence of a spouse and family suggested permanence. Moreover, children born in America to these families could possibly claim rights which America was unwilling to confer. Accordingly, then, white America tended to view all Asian women as prostitutes. What other function could they have in America but to sexually service the disproportionately large number of Chinese men living in Chinatown's bachelor society? The Chinese girl's portrayal in *Old San Francisco* provides an early popular stereotype of the sexually available Asian woman, while her death effectively removes the vessel which could bring into this white world yet another member of the yellow horde. Indeed, the girl's removal also eliminates the type of instrument by which grossly disfigured character types such as Buckwell and his dwarf brother might enter the world through the mixing of the races. Only disfigured characters whose deformations could be called upon to serve in the gross definition of difference could be allowed to survive into the future of San Francisco; Chinese characters representing fully psychologized individuals were eliminated.

So, throughout her career Anna May Wong's Asian screen characters died, or at best survived to live out clearly defined marginal roles. By age fifteen, she had already helped to establish the dying Asian female through her role as Lotus Flower in *The Toll of the Sea* (1922). With only a slight reworking of the Long/Belasco/Puccini butterfly construction, Lotus Flower commits suicide by walking into the sea after surrendering her son to the father's American family. Just one year earlier, Wong had been listed as Lotus Blossom among the supporting credits of *Shame* (1921), which featured the threat of miscegenation and a Chinese opium-smuggling scheme. Her most famous silent-film role was in *The Thief of Bagdad* (1924), in which she plays both Mongol slave and spy.

Playing Hue Fei opposite Marlene Dietrich in *Shanghai Express* (1932), Wong portrayed a character predetermined by American filmography: the criminally complicit, sexually available Asian woman, not to be trusted. Hue Fei unabashedly accepts the marginal position of prostitute and murders a man after he rapes her. The killing allows the plot to proceed to a satisfactory conclusion. Her victim, Harry Chang (Warner Oland), is once again a Chinese man who can pass as white; this time he also serves the Chinese Communist party and clearly is worthy of death. Shanghai Lily (Marlene Dietrich) returns to Captain Donald Harvey, the love of her life, while Hue Fei returns to Shanghai, presumably to resume her life as a prostitute, though nothing is said of what is to become of her. The Wong character is merely cut adrift.

Warner Oland, the actor whose character Anna May Wong murders in *Shanghai Express*, had appeared previously with her many times. Indeed, a year earlier Oland had played her father in *Daughter of the Dragon* (1931). Wong plays Princess Ling Moy, an exotic dancer who learns that she is the daughter of the infamous dragon Fu Manchu. As he is about to die, Ling Moy is compelled by mysterious, almost genetic filial obligation to complete the revenge which her father has just failed to accomplish. Unfortunately, she falls in love with the son of her white victim. Drugged, she is forced into continuing in her murderous plot. Ling Moy stands poised with knife in hand ready to strike when she is finally shot dead by Ah Kee, a Chinese detective working for Scotland Yard. How convenient that the Chinese should kill off their own — it is a sort of representational genocide in which white America, despite its authorial role, can absolve itself of any connection. Of course, both Fu Manchu and dragon-lady characters such as Ling Moy would live on to die and die again, forever reinscribing the dangers of the Orient and miscegenation while spiraling through seemingly endless cycles of death.

Ironically, with the temporary death of his Fu Manchu character in *Daughter of the Dragon*, Warner Oland would go on to play the kind of "good" Oriental detective who kills Princess Moy. Before his sudden death six years later in 1938, Oland would perform the lead in some sixteen Charlie Chan films, establishing the good Oriental detective, with his mysterious crime-solving ways, as a new order of Asian representation. Oland's successors include Sidney Toler and Roland Winters. Ranging through forty-six films, the Charlie Chan character became institutionalized as clever but sexless, even effeminate.

Some of America's most influential film and theatre figures can be counted among the makers of productions which feature dead or dying Asians. Along with D. W. Griffith's Chink in *Broken Blossoms*, Frank Capra's *The Bitter Tea of General Yen* (1932) is worthy of note. Famous for such optimistic films as *Miracle on 34th Street* (1947) and *It's a Wonderful Life* (1946), Capra held a dim view of the mixing of the races. General Yen (Nils Asther), an infamous Chinese warlord, captures Megan Davis (Barbara Stanwyck) as she tries to rescue orphaned children threatened by revolutionary chaos. Fluent in English, a sophisticated and erudite individual, Yen falls in love as he attempts to seduce his fascinating white captive. The Barbara Stanwyck character seems gradually to come

Daughter of the Dragon. *Wisconsin Center for Film and Theatre Research, State Historical Society of Wisconsin.*

around, even to the extent of fantasizing General Yen as lover. But audiences of the day would not be kind to the notion of miscegenation, so General Yen dutifully drinks his bitter poisoned tea and dies, freeing the woman to return to the missionary to whom she is betrothed. Despite his well-known optimistic films, Capra was uniquely qualified for later work as a producer of many racist, government-sponsored anti-Japanese propaganda films during World War II.

By refusing the potential for Asian propagation on Western soil, the stage and film deaths serve to deny or problematize the future of any progeny that might result from miscegenous relationships. Indeed, this denial persists to this day. In the television series *Raven* (1992), the action centers on the white male lead character's continuing weekly search for his absent child, the product of an interracial relationship. Conveniently, the Asian mother died during delivery. During the course of his

The Bitter Tea of General Yen. *Wisconsin Center for Film and Theatre Research, State Historical Society of Wisconsin.*

search, the white man must overcome evil Asian gangsters without ever actually dealing with the absence that provides motivation for the series. He will likely never find this child, for when he does the story will be finished.

The original desire to contain and control the Chinese in particular and the Asian in general, although now obscured, somehow maintains a compelling representational power over newly constructed images. While the initial intention had been to warn spectators against miscegenation, the recent versions seem to accept the product of mixed-race relations while desiring to keep the alien half of the relationship which produced the progeny contained, preferably dead. But then this had been the case from the very beginning. The film *Old San Francisco* ends with a look into the future of a glorious, apparently white city after the death of the threatening Chinese. The future of the villain's clearly disfigured dwarf brother remains ambiguous. While Buckwell's fate is sealed, the futures of the progeny of Cho-Cho-San, Lotus Flower, and Miss Saigon are left suspended, to provide potential sites for the controlled construction of more disfigured characters like Buckwell and his dwarf brother. Moreover, the tendency to arrest development or to absent the child completely suggests the presence of a problem from which America would prefer to avert its eyes — or at the least not deal with seriously.[4] In any case, it is clear that in the popular consciousness at least, Asianness has fled from the real into the realm of representational desire. Yet clearly this is the path that mediated desire must follow to be successful. Unfortunately, in such renderings as *Madama Butterfly, Old San Francisco, Daughter of the Dragon, The Bitter Tea of General Yen, The Lady from Yesterday*, and *Miss Saigon*, the constructed Orient carries with it an element of self-destruction. But then again, to repeat Catherine Clement, only through its death or self-effacement does Asia become real for the Western spectator.

8

Eugene O'Neill's
Marco Millions
Desiring Marginality and the
Dematerialization of Asia

During the late nineteenth century, American theatrical representations of Asia in general, and the Chinese in particular, usually deployed characters consisting entirely of fetishized aspects of difference, as if to remind the viewer that the constructed foreign qualities of the Orient could never be assimilated into the American geography. One need only look to the "Chinese" ninnies in the almost ubiquitous revivals of Lindsay and Crouse's *Anything Goes* (1934) for a brief and embarrassingly comic reminder of how even late twentieth-century audiences have viewed the Orient. However, by the beginning of the twentieth century, the Chinese also came to be portrayed in their exotic, foreign, homeland locales by writers who chose to believe that Asians could not be assimilated, not even into an imaginary American realm.

Such portrayals of the Chinese employed some subtle displacements, particularly among writers who would use the Chinese character for seriously intended projects. Clearly, Eugene O'Neill's *Marco Millions* (1927) must be counted among them. The play was written between the summer of 1923 and January 1925, when the copyright was issued. At an intermediate stage in October 1924, O'Neill recorded that in *Marco Millions* he had written to his surprise "two good long plays of 2½ hours each — at least."[1] Finally cut and integrated into a standard-length play and published in April 1927, *Marco Millions* did not receive its first staging until 9 January 1928 at the Guild Theatre in New York. Brooks Atkinson's review of the opening-night performance offers the following summary:

> Ten scenes of "Marco Millions" record the journey of the merchant Polos through Persia and India to Cathay. Under a special dispensation from the Great Kaan, who is fascinated by Marco's lack of perception, the younger Marco goes through the kingdom, organizing furiously with the high spirits and the arrogant self-assurance of a bustling business man. In everything material he succeeds with a brilliance matched only by his cheap ethics. He fails only in awareness of the ancient culture of Cathay and in Princess Kukachin's despairing love. Acting under orders of the Great Kaan, he takes her out to Persia in a voyage two years long. Never once does her unselfish affection burn through the greedy, egotistical shell of his character. Mr. O'Neill chronicles all this in terms of emotional tragedy as well as satire. While Marco is swilling wine and costly viands at a banquet in Venice, and saluting his fat, stupid bride, boasting and gorging, the Great Kaan sits disconsolate in his throne room, eating out his heart for his home-sick, love-sick granddaughter, who could never speak her love. Marco's "spiritual hump" had been, strangely enough, their undoing.[2]

In *Marco Millions* O'Neill sought to contrast the obsessive materialism of an American Babbitt-like character with a positive representation of a historicized, romantic China. Despite the clear comic intent of the piece, one might assume that the portrayal of the Chinese, even if not "realistic," would at least be "positive" within this framework. Indeed, because O'Neill clearly presents the Venetians in a less than flattering light, this may seem at first to be the case. In both visual appearance and stage action Marco and his uncles do not come off well. Costumes for Polo and company made the three appear almost buffoonish in the 1928

Marco Millions. *University of Wisconsin Libraries.*

production. Robert Coleman of the *New York Daily Mirror* described
Marco as a "cheap, soulless, handshaking, baby-kissing politician."[3]
Similarly, Alexander Woolcott of *The World* called Marco the "eternal
portrait of the globe-trotting business man who takes notes on everything and sees nothing, who memorizes all he hears and learns
nothing."[4]

Though O'Neill succeeded in portraying the Venetian trading family
satirically, the construction of his Orient proved problematic. His characterizations of the Chinese are intended to show subtle differences between the West and his Orient.

Against the subtlety of Kublai, the Great Kaan of Cathay, and his
poetic wisdom, Mr. O'Neill has set the crude, braggart character of
Marco, greedy, expeditious, material-minded and obtuse. In all the
gorgeous variety of scenes in the throne-room or on the extravagant

ships bearing the love-sick Princess out to Persia, Mr. O'Neill has been specific by contrast rather than by statement. Yet the implications of his bizarre pageant are always articulate and forceful.[5]

While the playwright's intentions might appear obvious, Atkinson's assertion that all the implications of O'Neill's "bizarre pageant are always articulate and forceful" seems much too positive. For, while O'Neill's deployment of the Orient is intended to provide positive contrast to the blind materialism of the Western characters, the manner in which he constructs the Orient creates an internal tension with the potential to overturn his project.

Through the use of recurring scenes in the middle part of the first act, O'Neill hoped to provide Marco's decline into callousness with a universal quality.[6] If this is true, an odd tension emerges between O'Neill's desire for the wisdom of his Orient and the Polo characters he sends to the East to carry out his project. To begin with, if Asia is the site for the righteous ancient wisdom which O'Neill would have us accept, it is curious that as he progresses eastward Marco becomes more hardened, and the prostitutes more aggressive and cynical, which suggests a female Asian sexual threat. Marco's pattern of resistance to O'Neill's Oriental prostitute reinscribes the earlier construction of the sexually available Asian woman. Notwithstanding the passive women nursing children as well as lovers embracing in tableaux, Marco, after the encounters with the prostitutes, could not possibly be interested in anyone other than his bovine Christian Venetian betrothed. Within this pattern, Kukachin is imprisoned. She is trapped within the broad array of that Western catalogue which lists the Orient as passive, weak, and feminine or androgynous, while the West is viewed as active, dominant, and male. For her to be anything other than passive and distant in her unrequited love for Marco would cause her to be grouped with the sexually available Asian prostitute.

The neutralized Asian woman, placed within a context devoid of European female characters who might prove a sexual threat, served to render O'Neill's Orient a place without even the potential for romantic involvement. O'Neill's construction, of course, draws focus to the con-

Marco Millions. *University of Wisconsin Libraries.*

trast between what could be called an oddly ironic sentimental Oriental
love and Marco's very businesslike "love" relationship with Donata.
Save for the sexually available Asian woman, this constitution of Asian
love neutralizes any possible active role for Asian characters.

There is also a disturbing sameness about the manner in which
O'Neill animates his Orient. O'Neill's efforts to trivialize or deny differences between various Eastern cultures seem more successful than the
scenes in the first act that he designed to provide a sense of universality.
He suggests, for example, that Persia is little different from India. Save
for variations in the religious architecture and the presence of the dis-
dainful snake charmer in India, O'Neill would have us believe that the
frozen background characters in both scenes are somehow universal:
"Only their eyes move, staring fixedly but indifferently at the Polos." In the first
production of *Marco Millions,* this problem was aggravated by the need
to eliminate a scene set in Mongolia which provided a transition between
India and the Polos' arrival in China. The net effect is a conflation of
every geographic setting from Persia to China into a single awkwardly

defined narrative space of otherness called China, where the main action of this Oriental play occurs. Within this place O'Neill seemed not to differentiate between Mongol and Chinese, as all seem to live and work together happily. Yet even Marco Polo's memoirs (O'Neill's notes claim a careful reading of this text),[7] suggest a significantly different situation:

> And you should know that all the Cathayans detested the Great Kaan's rule because he set over them governors who were Tartars, or still more frequently Saracens, and these they could not endure for they were treated by them just like slaves. You see the Great Kaan had not succeeded to the dominion of Cathay by hereditary right, but held it by conquest; and thus having no confidence in the natives, he put all authority into the hands of Tartars, Saracens, or Christians who were attached to his household and devoted to his service, and were foreigners in Cathay.[8]

Eugene O'Neill's Marco travels to China to fill the Great Kaan's request for representatives of the wisdom of the West. In an interesting self-reflexive fashion, Eugene O'Neill himself turned to the East in hope of locating a philosophy to satisfy his personal quest for significance in life. Accordingly, the play speaks the desire of O'Neill's imaginary Asia through the language of the West. Kublai, realizing that his granddaughter has fallen hopelessly in love with Marco, declares, "Life is so stupid, it is mysterious," and later threatens to have Marco killed.[9] But his advisor, Chu-Yin, the wise Oriental forever spouting aphorisms, admonishes in soothing tones and reminds the ruler:

> The noble man ignores self. The wise man ignores action. His truth acts without deeds. His knowledge venerates the unknowable. To him birth is not the beginning nor is death the end. [*Kublai's head bends in submission. Chu-Yin continues tenderly.*] I feel there are tears in your eyes. The Great Kaan, Ruler of the World, may not weep. (97)

Similarly, Chu-Yin calms an angry Kukachin by suggesting that she have a "little sleep, Princess, and you will be beautiful. The old dream passes. Sleep and awake in the new. Life is perhaps most wisely regarded as a bad dream between two awakenings, and everyday is a life in miniature" (98). O'Neill believes that for his Oriental, the life of the mind transcends the everyday.

Still, the Great Kaan is after all human, and he finds himself torn between the desire to act forcefully on his granddaughter's behalf and the mandate to follow the supposed path of Asian wisdom, passivity and avoidance:

> She will die. Why is this? What purpose can it serve? My hideous suspicion is that God is only an infinite, insane energy which creates and destroys without other purpose than to pass eternity in avoiding thought. Then the stupid man becomes the Perfect Incarnation of Omnipotence and the Polos are the true children of God. . . . I begin to resent life as the insult of an ignoble inferior with whom it is a degradation to fight! (134)

To his credit O'Neill did not resort to the use of pidgin English for his Asian characters. Most of his predecessors in American playwriting had employed a curiously degraded English for great comic effect to suggest how Asians would seek to express themselves in their adopted tongue. O'Neill's use of English is entirely appropriate because the ideas the characters express are uniquely his own American notion of what constitutes Asia. It seems, however, that ultimately O'Neill finds his Oriental philosophy intriguing and novel but less than satisfactory, for he has Kukachin drowsily declare: "Your wisdom makes me sleepy" (98). And, finally, even the Great Kaan attacks the wisdom of the Orient: "Your words are hollow echoes of the brain. Do not wound me with wisdom. Speak to my heart!" (153).

While the materialistic West is shown to be "unromantic," O'Neill's detached Oriental "wisdom" proves impotent in the face of the Western desire for money and power. As Marco proclaims: "I kept my nose to the grindstone every minute. [*Proudly.*] And I got results. I don't mind telling you, Donata, I'm worth over two millions!" (141–142). Although the dominant materialistic Western position is clearly not a utopian enterprise to be sought after, the apparently privileged imaginary Orient that O'Neill creates beyond the margins of the West is also finally dismissed by its dominant practitioners in the play, Kublai and Kukachin.

In seeking to create a marginal utopian Orient beyond his realm of experience, O'Neill fell into a trap. Virginia Floyd observed that despite "Kukachin's passion and Kublai's heartbreak at her death, the play lacks warmth and emotional intensity. The numerous scenes and characters, the panoramic passing of time and peoples, seems to preclude a sensitive treatment" (301). Indeed, the effect of the spectacular scenery and the almost epic displacement of the viewer through a series of some ten episodes is significant. Although Percy Hammond of the *New York Herald Tribune* complained that the Guild Theatre performance was "warped a little by its eight intermissions,"[10] Atkinson reported that the opening production "pours from the stage in rapturous beauty. . . . The telling of the story involves theatrical richness, a kaleidoscope of scenes. Costumes of surpassing patterns and colors, processionals, chorals, mobs, bells, gongs, bands, a fury of wild voices, dark brooding silhouettes against the sky, and brief passages of exalting discourse on grand themes."[11]

O'Neill offers his construction of China to spectators in much the same way a tourist might describe the high points of his summer holiday, memories of a "heathen" place never experienced.[12] Significantly, O'Neill's list of characters for *Marco Millions* catalogues all non-Western figures in the play under the general heading of "heathens." In the foreword to the published volume of *Marco Millions*, O'Neill decried the fact that Marco Polo of Venice "dictated the book of his travels but left the traveller out. He was no author. He stuck to a recital of what he considered facts" (5). In his play, O'Neill inserts the viewer into the powerful position of the tourist before whom he parades the carefully selected "high points" of an imaginary philosophical excursion to China. The discourse of the Orient, of the Other as articulated through the tourist culture's vision is in many ways typical.[13] The Orient is rarely given voice, for the moment the Other speaks, it becomes a threat. As with O'Neill's predecessors, the capturing/controlling gaze serves as the mechanism for manipulation. The montage of fetishized traits typical of nineteenth-century American portrayals of the Orient is replaced by a rapid displacement of the viewer through a sequence of locales peopled by spectacular mannikins.[14] Through this process, the Orient is displaced into the space of representation as white actors pretend to be Chinese — and almost immediately again displaced into the void or darkness which emerges between the numerous episodes of the play. Thus, just as Marco and family move from one setting to another, suitcases in hand, without substantive interaction, so the audience comes away with nothing.

In designing his imaginary realm called China, O'Neill fell into the trap of stereotyping the Orient. China disintegrated into representation, displacing/erasing the reality. Accordingly, like the tourist whose appearance materially alters the foreign terrain visited, O'Neill's Venetian adventurer remains unchanged, while the place called Asia becomes an infantilized and "perfect" but finally empty imaginary locale — even the fictional Marco Polo walks out puzzled in the play's epilogue.

9

Disfiguring
The Castle of Fu Manchu
Racism Reinscribed in the
Playground of the Postmodern

Joel was a janitor at the Gizmonic Institute, an establishment for the study of gizmos. "Just a face in a red jumpsuit, he did a good job cleaning up the place," but his bosses "didn't like him so they shot him into space." As he circles the planet his bosses torment him by beaming up movies, "the worst we can find." Because Joel used parts from the control panel to create a group of robot friends to keep him company, he has lost control over the circumstances of the film viewing. Accordingly, he and his robot companions can do little more than sit in front of and comment aloud on the screened films. And comment aloud they do, with a vengeance. This provides the context for the *Mystery Science Theatre 3000* which airs on Comedy Central, a cable television channel available nationally in many markets.

The feature film offered on 17 January 1992 was *The Castle of Fu Manchu* (1968), starring Christopher Lee as the infamous Fu Manchu and Tsai Chin as his daughter, Lin Tang. In her autobiography, Tsai Chin, who appeared in many of the Fu Manchu films, summarized the typical plot:

Apart from the name changes, the plots were all identical: perhaps that explains why I did not bother to read the script when I came to do the fifth film. Fu wants to conquer the world, forcing a Western scientist to assist him. The white and noble scientist always refuses to co-operate until Fu abducts his beautiful daughter. Then the scientist pretends to relent before destroying his evil opponent. End of picture — though as the credits roll, the menacing voice of Fu Manchu is heard warning his Western cinema audience that worse is yet to come.[1]

In *The Castle of Fu Manchu*, the terror which Fu threatens to visit upon the earth is a chemically induced freezing of the seas of the world, leaving death and chaos in its wake. To demonstrate his power, Fu creates an iceberg in the Caribbean to sink a pleasure-cruise liner and later destroys a dam in Turkey. Professor Herakles is the unwilling scientist he hopes to press into service, and Nayland Smith, the Scotland Yard inspector called in to bring about a rescue.

After Fu Manchu sinks the cruise liner, Nayland Smith must abruptly end his vacation and return to London, where he will lead the effort to once again defeat the infamous Oriental tyrant. Fu Manchu's broadcast message to the world is ominous: "in the Caribbean Sea, I gave a demonstration of the new and destructive weapon I possess. The world has two weeks to comply, obedience to my orders or obliteration. If disaster is to be avoided, I shall insist upon complete cooperation. I shall give no further warning, but unless the heads of state of the major powers are prepared to meet my demands, in fourteen days from now, I shall strike." While the demands are unclear, Smith declares the threat to be one of "almost biblical" proportions.

The scene now shifts to Istanbul, where Fu Manchu's daughter, Lin Tang (Tsai Chin), and Lisa, a mysterious woman who always appears cross-dressed in male Turkish apparel, arrange a meeting with Lisa's master Omar Pasha, who agrees to help Fu Manchu capture the castle of the Governor of Anatolia in exchange for "one half of the world opium trade." Once the castle is taken and the Governor beheaded by Lin Tang, Fu Manchu reveals his intention to dominate the world from this newly acquired real estate on the shores of the Bosporus. But Professor Herakles, the scientist who holds the secret formula for Fu's dastardly plan, is terminally ill and in need of a heart transplant. So, Dr. Kessler, an experimental heart transplant expert, along with his colleague, Dr. Ingrid Cox, are kidnapped in London and transported to Turkey to perform the needed surgical procedure.

Nayland Smith, who happened to be waiting in Kessler's inner office during the kidnapping, concludes that Fu Manchu must be behind both the surgeon's disappearance and the news accounts of violence on the Bosporus. Reasoning that Fu Manchu needs the site for access to vast quantities of water to carry out his nefarious scheme of world domination, Smith immediately departs for Turkey. In Istanbul, Omar Pasha, now suspicious of Fu Manchu's intentions, agrees to help Smith in toppling the Oriental threat.

When Dr. Kessler refuses to perform the surgery on Professor Herakles, Fu provides another demonstration of his watery destructive powers on a dam and finally threatens the life of the surgeon's female colleague. After this threat, they undertake the surgery. Professor Herakles miraculously recovers, the secret formula is extorted, and Fu Manchu appears poised to carry out his plan. Speaking from his castle in Anatolia, the Asian half of Turkey, he warns, "if the governments of all the nations do not accept my terms in four days' time, I will bring desolation to mankind." Omar Pasha is captured and killed. Chinese hordes dressed in black attack his encampment and reports say that Nayland Smith and all of Pasha's men are dead.

In the final scenes of the film, Dr. Kessler uses explosive acid from the operating room to break out of his cell. He and Dr. Cox escape through water tunnels which lead to the sea. Fu Manchu floods these tunnels in preparation for his cataclysmic attack on the world, as Nayland Smith swims into the castle to rescue Professor Herakles and Lisa. But when they emerge into the sunshine, Lisa goes back into the tunnels in an ill-fated attempt to save her master, Omar Pasha. Lisa drowns, and the castle of Fu Manchu inexplicably explodes along with the tyrant's hopes of world domination. However, as noted earlier by Chin, when the credits roll, Fu Manchu reminds the audience in an ominous voice that "the world will hear from me again."

The film is rendered a substandard product by directorial problems, disruptions in narrative logic, and technical flaws. Accordingly, it is worthy of *Mystery Science Theatre 3000*, where the producers strive to air only "the worst we can find."

Fu Manchu is clearly a reinscription of the evil Chinaman who can compete with whites in a fashion not unlike both Slim Chunk Pin in Grimm's play and Buckwell in *Old San Francisco*. The film, inspired by Sax Rohmer's early twentieth-century novels, resurrects the evil Asian master criminal of the nineteenth century. Interestingly, in *The Castle of Fu Manchu*, this evil Chinese character actually does very little. Indeed, like his predecessors, he mostly threatens while his underlings carry out his wishes, which in turn require his Anglo adversaries to respond with frantic actions bordering on hysteria. This ability to provoke hysteria reinscribes the Asian threat to the orderly progress of the West. Hysteria and chaos, then, result from the passivity of Asia, personified by this regal Mandarin whose threats are nothing without his mindless, visually neutralized yellow horde.

Whereas in the film *Old San Francisco* Buckwell preys upon his Chinese brethren and the whites of California, Fu Manchu not only threatens the Anglo Western world but murders his Turkish coconspirators. Indeed, both the evil Fu Manchu and his Turkish counterpart, Omar Pasha, emerge as heartless evil leaders who kill their own at the slightest provocation. Curiously, the only characters who actually encounter physical damage during the course of the narrative are the Orientals, the Turks and the Chinese. The internecine warfare that breaks out between the criminal Chinese and Turkish factions suggests that neither are civilized enough to compete with the moral West. Even the ailing Professor Herakles comes out ahead when he receives a heart transplant requiring the sacrifice of a member of one of the evil factions. By the end of the film all of the Asians have been disposed of, while the whites survive, despite the voice of Fu Manchu threatening a future return engagement.

To drive home the weaknesses of the film, the producers of *Mystery*

Silhouetted in the lower right-hand corner of the TV screen, Joel and his robot companions offer nonstop commentaries on the movies they — and the Mystery Science Theatre 3000 *viewers — are forced to watch each week. Comedy Central.*

Science Theatre 3000 provide a running commentary throughout the screening. Seen in silhouette between the film image and the spectator, Joel and his two robot companions offer what could be characterized as a stinging Brechtian counterpoint to the ongoing screen narrative. The television viewer is provided with an experience like that of sitting behind three noisy critics in a movie house. With the audio volume of the commentary often louder than that of the film itself, the already internally flawed and disrupted narrative is further distorted by a continuing leering comic verbal attack. Fu Manchu warns the world of his two-week deadline to comply, and a voice-over robot commentator muses aloud over whether "that's fourteen business days or what." When a character arriving on his bicycle is asked, "What [business] brings you here?" his response is obliterated by Joel's voice saying "my bicycle." A filmic moment offered dimly in half-light reminds one commentator of "a *Nova* special on conception." A street scene with Turks wearing fezzes inspires this voice-over: "looks like a meeting of the Shriner mafia."

Beyond the sophomoric wit, rich intertextual potentials emerge as the voice-overs at once both amuse and subvert the construction of viable characters. Stereotyping of Turks collapses into a Jimi Hendrix lyric when Omar Pasha looks up from his hookah to meet Lin Tang for the first time: "Oh wow, I'm so high, excuse me while I kiss the sky." What Pasha actually says is lost, disfigured by the voice-over. Fu Manchu notes that the cross-dressed Lisa "fights like a man," which inspires a line from a Bob Dylan lyric: "but she breaks just like a little girl." At various points in the narrative, the three vocal critics seem to compete for the wittiest response. As Lin Tang observes the surgical procedure before a stark white background which produces a mug-shot effect, one commentator, playing off the visual pun, adopts a Detective Joe Friday voice from the television series *Dragnet* to say that she had been convicted of impersonating Marlo Thomas, star of the television series *That Girl*. Competing with this is yet another mock voice-over of Lin Tang claiming to be Suzy Wong, the fictional prostitute from a feature film of the same name. As the camera pulls back, two Chinese male characters come into view, and for each in turn a commentator likewise claims the coveted Suzy Wong identity. Such gender play, which appears through-out the piece, collapses into racial aporia when one commentator iden-tifies the tall white actor playing Fu Manchu (Christopher Lee) with Kareem Abdul-Jabbar, former basketball star of the L.A. Lakers. Throughout such voice-over wordplay, sexual suggestion gives way to mock censorship when Fu Manchu and Lin Tang must make a hasty exit: "How about a quickie . . . [pause] for a cocktail that is."

In addition, geography is obliterated when a view of London is cov-ered by a voice saying, "meanwhile in downtown Ames, Iowa." Throughout the film, similar shots are refigured by references to the Wisconsin Dells, Chicago, St. Paul, and Wyoming, despite the fact that the locations on the screen are clearly intended to be European or Asian. Employing this domestication of exotic locale, Fu Manchu's throne room in his newly acquired Anatolian castle becomes Ivana Trump's bathroom.

For the sake of commercial breaks, the already internally flawed nar-rative of the film is further almost arbitrarily divided into nine segments. Between four and six advertisements appear as intertexts to each of the nine film narrative sections. The advertisements attempt to sell every-thing from Dial soap to Sassoon hair care products, Advil headache medication, Hall's cough medicine, Pert shampoo, Bic pens, Hidden Val-ley salad dressing, Thighmaster exercise equipment, Pop Secret pop-corn, and some thirty other products. These nine ruptures of the cine-matic narrative serve to further alienate the spectator from a film already marked as a product of a bygone racist era.

In addition, with virtually every scene of the film commented upon, the overall effect of this continuous comic critique is the total subversion of any possible narrative development. One understands what the story is supposed to be but ends up wondering what the next interesting com-mentator joke will be. Interest in the conflict, then, has in a sense been displaced from the cinematic narrative line into seemingly almost ran-dom sequence of the commentary. This alternative horizon of expecta-tions proceeds not in total chaos but with an internal logic all its own.

Beyond the voice-over commentary, Joel, his robot companions, and his land-based tormentors stage several sketches. Situated between the filmic narrative segments and the commercial breaks, the sketches serve to provide opportunities for character definition and for editorial commentary. In the first of the sketches, the earthbound "scientists," who have exiled Joel into space, reinforce their continuing intention to torment him by transmitting the worst films they can find. Accordingly, they inform Joel and his robot company that *The Castle of Fu Manchu* is a film so bad that it will curl their shoes as well as their toes! Later sketches make clear the constructed tensions that exist between the captors on earth and the captives. Both parties, it seems, understand the racist nature of the film being aired. The captors derive a sadistic pleasure from the pained responses of the prisoners. The orbiting commentators, unable to control the means of their viewing, have no recourse but to verbally disfigure the distasteful narrative which they must witness. The spectator, then, constructs a frame around all this in an attempt to achieve meaning.

These radical displacements serve to highlight the retrogressively racist tendencies of the film. For instance, after Omar Pasha agrees to aid in Fu Manchu's scheme in return for control of one-half of the world's opium trade, the film narrative breaks for the second set of commercials. Before the ads appear, however, one of Joel's robot companions reads "The Miss Saigon Syndrome: An Editorial by Crow T. Robot":

I can no longer sit idly by on my little robot haunches and watch Caucasian actors be continually cast in non-Caucasian roles. Christopher Lee's portrayal of Fu Manchu is a crystalline example of the phenomenon I've titled "Bad Actors, Bad Decisions." This insidious tradition of casting has formed a psychological backdrop in which we play out the insignificant comings and goings of our daily lives. Let me, Crow T. Robot, pull back the curtain to reveal the lie on which your lie is based. Signpost number one on your road to discovery, George Pal's enchanting *7 Faces of Dr. Lao*. Would it shock you to know that all seven faces were played by white musical theatre actor, Tony Randall? Wake up people, that's seven examples right there! Now you're saying to yourself, please Mr. Robot, carrier of the gleaming sword of truth, don't spoil the shining obelisk of Sunday afternoon enjoyment, Charlie Chan. Sorry, it's my job. Charlie Chan is a Swede named Warner Oland. Crow, stop now, you're woozy. No! The truth is a runaway train. Who's that playing an Asian in *The Teahouse of the August Moon*? It's your precious method actor Marlon Brando! . . . So in conclusion, Cameron Mackintosh: "Bite me!"

Several times during the course of his speech, the robot breaks into tears, and his companions console and encourage him by claiming the spectators "love your acerbic editorials." Their earthbound monitors note that their captives are experiencing "deep pain" and congratulate themselves as worthy of a "Nobel Prize for Evil." The ludicrous notion of such a prize is immediately displaced by a Comedy Central commercial featuring President George Bush as a comedian in a forthcoming special. Following ads for Pert Plus shampoo, Bic shavers, *JFK* (the film), and Thighmaster, Omar Pasha's men are seen aiding in Fu Manchu's assault on the castle of the Anatolian governor. One subsequent sketch mocks the Turkish stereotype, as Joel and his robot companions all appear on flying carpets, while yet another offers a comic cartoon rendering of the birth of the Fu Manchu name. Such ruptures in the narrative of *The Castle of Fu Manchu* are typical of the two-hour *Mystery Science Theatre 3000* program.

The intention is clear. The rapid displacement from Pasha's agreement to aid in Fu Manchu's scheme into the editorial that attacks the film as an example of racist casting in the industry makes explicit the position of the producers. By attacking the racist film, the earthbound monitors remind the spectator that the film is so bad that it inflicts pain, thus making the editorial all the more valiant. Tsai Chin thought so little of this film that she omitted it from her filmography. Still, one does not walk away from this program angry with the representational institutions which produced *The Castle of Fu Manchu.*

As the program unfolds, one initially shifts attention from the film narrative to the voice-over commentary, and later still to the apparent political correctness of the producers' stance on the casting practices behind such projects. This in turn begins to influence the reception of the film as the spectator becomes increasingly complicit in the comic commentary which seeks to disfigure the narrative. To completely resist the voice-over commentary in favor of the filmic narrative is not only politically incorrect, aligning one with the evil monitors on earth, it is also problematic because of the film's low production values. Still, as the commentary is dependent upon the film text, spectator attention eventually settles into a reading that moves rapidly back and forth between both texts. Accordingly, the viewer can check the efficacy of each emergent commentary with the film narrative.

The displacement between commentary and text would seem to provide the much-sought-after Brechtian space for reflection to allow the spectator opportunity to judge for herself the validity of the positions deployed in this two-hour text. And, this may well have been Comedy Central's intent. Unfortunately, Brecht's modernist model for changing the social text is here crushed by the play of the postmodern. The displacement out of the narrative is itself disfigured because the play of commentary occurs at such a rapid pace. The spectator is rarely able to complete the thought inspired by the voice-over before both the filmic text and its nemesis move on to another scene. Indeed, not only does the text jump from film narrative to commentary, the sketches, juxtaposed with commercials, create ruptures which can displace the spectator all the way into the kitchen. Finally, the intertextual play between the nine internally awkward film segments of *The Castle of Fu Manchu*, the ongoing voice-over commentary, five sketches, and forty-seven advertisements offered through nine commercial breaks reduces the entire two-hour text to a rapidly moving sequence whose only closure is achieved when the time allotted to the event is used up.

Accordingly, spectators are not likely to sit through the entire program. A close reading of this two-hour text becomes quite an intense experience as the relations among commercials, sketches, and filmic narrative combine for a richly dense intertextual web that approaches the absurd.

Through all of this, though, three aspects of the text persist: (1) the variety of the high production value commercials; (2) the incredible staying power of Fu Manchu, who despite the chaos of the two-hour program insists that he will return to threaten the world again; and (3) the virtuosity of the commentators, whose apparent quick-witted ability to disfigure the film as it unfolds is worthy of applause. The commercials, with their relatively high production values when contrasted with the remainder of the two-hour visual text, make clear the material concerns behind the event. The virtuosity of the commentators requires more interrogation. The issue of virtuosity is addressed directly by the last sketch of the program. The earthbound captors, while applauding Joel and company's witty commentary, set out to prove that they too can produce comic voice-overs. In an amusing deconstruction of the process, they rescreen clips from *The Castle of Fu Manchu* and attempt to make funny observations. They of course fail, and the audience can conclude that the orbiting characters are indeed virtuous voice-over speakers. But the voice-over, like the voice of god or conscience, reminds the audience of both the virtuosity of the commentators and Fu Manchu's threat of present and future terror. And so spectators are reminded that while *Mystery Science Theatre 3000* may eventually face cancellation, the racist construction of the Asian archcriminal will likely make many return engagements.

Through *Mystery Science Theatre 3000*'s staging of *The Castle of Fu Manchu*, both the racist agency and its constructed evil Asian figure are attacked. Yet in the end neither appears damaged, for it is only postmodern play in the service of the consumer. The rapid displacing structure deployed for this staging of Fu Manchu claims to subvert the racist film's content but finally cannot overcome the history of reinscription protecting its stereotypical construction. The fear of the constructed evil Asian's amoral virtuosity, and his staying power, necessitates the rehearsal of his destruction, both in narrative and editorially. But these endless rehearsals at once force back into visibility the stereotype of disfigured/disfiguring Asian virtuosity while harboring its reinscription for future films.

10 Flawed Self-Representations

Authenticating Chinese American Marginality

One thinks one is tracing the outline of the thing's nature over and over again, and one is merely tracing around the frame through which we look at it. . . . A picture held us captive. And we could not get outside it, for it lay in our language and language seemed to repeat it to us inexorably.
— Ludwig Wittgenstein

The extent to which socially conscious drama can emerge from the morass of the bourgeois perception of the world is questionable at best.[1] Until recently, popular representations of Asian populations in America have remained at a level perhaps best described as stereotypical. Not until the new cultural awareness of the 1960s did this situation change as Asian American playwrights attempted to dispel stereotypes. As these playwrights emerged, the earlier comic or exotic treatments offered by whites were replaced by self-representations. Rarely popular with dominant-culture audiences, some of these plays did provide incisive examinations of what it is to be Chinese in a familiar yet alien land.

Important among these Asian American attempts to stage self-representations are a pair of works which seek to redefine Chinese American identity by confronting Anglo-American stereotyping of Asianness and the Orient. David Henry Hwang's *M. Butterfly* enjoyed a successful run on Broadway and won the Tony award for best American play of 1988.[2] In addition,

1988 saw successful runs of Philip Kan Gotanda's *Yankee Dawg You Die* in San Francisco, Los Angeles, and Chicago, with an off-Broadway production in New York during 1989.[3] Both plays feature Chinese characters as major figures and have received generally favorable press in America, though the authors of these plays claim to attack the established stereotypical representation of Asianness deployed by the traditional theatre. Accordingly, an awkward tension emerges between the popular acceptance of these works and the claim that the established stereotype is under attack.

Against the backdrop of the Vietnam War, China's Cultural Revolution, and the events of May 1968, *M. Butterfly* adapts the true-life tale of French diplomat René Bouriscot's twenty-year affair with a Beijing Opera performer, which resulted in the birth of a child and a trial for espionage. Through the character René Gallimard, Hwang reformulates Bouriscot's story. At Gallimard's trial it is revealed that his lover was not only a spy but a man. Accordingly, the audience is left to ponder how a sophisticated Western member of the diplomatic service could fall victim to so amusing a case of gender confusion. In order to set up this question, Hwang uses Puccini's *Madama Butterfly* as a point of departure for the diplomat's first encounter with his "mistress," which takes place at a performance of scenes from the Puccini opera in the German ambassador's residence in Beijing. Gallimard compliments the performance: "You were utterly convincing. It's the first time . . . I've seen the beauty of the story" (4). In response, Song Liling, the soon-to-be lover, assails the silliness of the Western stereotypes:

It's one of your favorite fantasies, isn't it? The submissive Oriental woman and the cruel white man . . . Consider it this way: what would you say if a blond homecoming queen fell in love with a short Japanese businessman? He treats her cruelly, then goes home for three years, during which time she prays to his picture and turns down marriage from a young Kennedy. Then, when she learns he has remarried, she kills herself. Now, I believe you would consider this girl to be a deranged idiot, correct? But because it's an Oriental who kills herself for a Westerner — ah! — you find it beautiful. (4)

Despite this harangue, Gallimard proceeds to entrap his "butterfly." We look on as he manipulates the emotions of Song Liling, all the while unaware that he himself has fallen into a trap of his own delusions regarding their relationship: "I stopped going to the opera, I didn't phone or write her . . . . and, as I wickedly refused to do so, I felt for the first time that rush of power — the absolute power of a man" (7). As Gallimard feels the "power of a man," Song explains: "All he wants is for her to submit. Once a woman submits, a man is always ready to become 'generous,'. . . . Now, if I can just present him with a baby. A Chinese baby with blond hair — he'll be mine for life!" (12). Gallimard's conquest of his butterfly complete, he applies his newfound wisdom to the conduct of international policy: "If the Americans demonstrate the will to win, the Vietnamese will welcome them into a mutually beneficial union . . . . Orientals will always submit to a greater force" (9–10). This of course was the mistake of the Vietnam war: "And somehow the American war went wrong. . . . Four hundred thousand dollars were being spent for every Viet Cong killed; so General Westmoreland's remark that the Oriental does not value life the way Americans do was oddly accurate. Why weren't the Vietnamese people giving in? Why were they content to die and die and die again?" (13).

Just as he had miscalculated the Vietnamese will to resist, so Gallimard had fallen hopelessly in love with a Song Liling created within his own imagination. When Song reveals his deception, Gallimard dismisses him: "You, you're as real as hamburger. Now get out! I have a date with my Butterfly." Gallimard explains that he is "a man who loved a woman created by a man. Everything else — simply falls short . . . . Tonight, I've finally learned to tell fantasy from reality. And, knowing the difference, I choose fantasy" (16). Gallimard's fantasy collapses the Orient into one indistinguishable mass, annihilating the differences between Chinese, Vietnamese, and Japanese. A vision of "slender women in chong sams and kimonos who die for the love of unworthy foreign devils. Who are born and raised to be the perfect women. Who take whatever punishment we give them, and bounce back, strengthened by love, unconditionally. It is a vision that has become my life" (16). As Gallimard's unworthy life interpenetrates that of his imaginary lover, he realizes that

M. Butterfly. *Joan Marcus.*

the only course open to him is the same as that chosen by Puccini's Cho-Cho-San: "Death with honor is better than life . . . with dishonor." When the diplomat commits suicide, Song, making explicit an ironic role reversal, declares Gallimard his "butterfly" as the lights fade to black (16).

Although Hwang's conflation of "imperialism, racism, and sexism"[4] may not always be clearly articulated in the development of Gallimard's flawed character, the indictment of the West is made explicit through Song's words: "The West has a sort of international rape mentality. . . . The West thinks of itself as masculine—big guns, big industry, big money—so the East is feminine—weak, delicate, poor . . . but good at art, and full of inscrutable wisdom—the feminine mystique. . . . Her mouth says no, but her eyes say yes. The West believes the East, deep down, *wants* to be dominated—because a woman can't think for herself" (15).

Resonances of Puccini's *Madama Butterfly* likewise permeate Philip Kan Gotanda's *Yankee Dawg You Die*. While Hwang's *M. Butterfly* cinematically spans some twenty years, the Gotanda piece examines the first year in the evolving relationship between an aspiring Japanese actor, Bradley Yamashita, and an older, more established "Chinese" actor. Gotanda's piece uses a stereotypical cinematic portrayal of a Japanese soldier to fix the general reception of Asianness in the popular consciousness. The opening scene of *Yankee Dawg You Die*, which attacks this standard portrayal of the Japanese, sets the tone for the rest of the play. The lead character in this piece, Vincent Chang, is a "Chinese" actor who is later revealed to be Japanese, having changed his name to find work after World War II. Accordingly, in the industry he is a Japanese man who pretended to be a Chinese actor so that he could get work portraying Japanese stereotypes.

If *M. Butterfly* merely attacks the Anglo-American system of representing Asianness, *Yankee Dawg You Die* reinforces the attack with a discussion of its impact. Bradley, for example, exposes the effects the cinematic castration of the Asian male has had on his life while accusing Vincent of perpetuating it:

Vincent . . . All that self hate . . . *Where does it begin?* You and your Charley Chop Suey roles. . . . you think every time you do one of those demeaning roles, the only thing lost is *your* dignity . . . Don't you see that every time you do a portrayal like that millions of people in movie theatres see it. *Believe* it. Every time you do any old stereotypic role just to pay the bills, you kill the right of some Asian child to be treated as a human being. To walk through the school yard and not be called a "chinaman gook" by some kid who saw the last Rambo film. (33–35)

Gotanda sensitively measures the depth of the Asian American desire to find role models. Bradley's misplaced identification with Neil Sedaka, a Jewish pop singer with a Japanese-sounding name, causes Yamashita to mistake him for America's first "Japanese American rock 'n roll star" (27). Finally, failing to locate an adequate human model for behavior, Gotanda seems to suggest that many Asian Americans have turned to the Japanese movie-monster Godzilla as a source of cultural pride and perhaps even identification (41–44). Gotanda's piece shifts back and forth between the issue of identifying proper role models on the one hand and the pragmatics of employment in the theatre/film industry on the other. Gotanda's desire to show "real" Asians is always suspended in tension with the Oriental stereotype required in the industry. And the stereotype usually wins out. Vincent's claim to being a "leading man" is repeatedly undercut by vignettes which display the mechanics of his stereotypical portrayals. Early on in the play, Bradley complains that the only roles open to Asians are "waiters, viet cong killers, chimpanzees, drug dealers, hookers, sexless houseboys . . . . They fucking cut off our balls and made us all houseboys on the evening soaps. 'Get your very own neutered, oriental houseboy!' " (36). Accordingly, this piece seems more overt than *M. Butterfly* in its attack on the theatrical institutions which work to subjugate the representations of the Orient.

Vincent makes clear his cognizance of his complicity within this theatrical institution by relating an early episode in the life of Martin Luther King: "They came and took him away. Told him they were going to kill him. He said he never felt more impotent, more like a slave than that

Yankee Dawg You Die. *Jennifer Girard.*

night. After that, he realized he had to fight not only the white man on the outside, but the slave inside of him . . . It is so easy to slip into the ching-chong chinaman" (60). Central to *Yankee Dawg You Die*, then, is the issue of how one must deal with this imperative which would seduce Asian Americans into the kind of cultural complicity required to "survive," to allow one to surrender to the cultural hegemony of Anglo dominance. In response to this issue Gotanda offers the contrast between the older Vincent Chang, who has "sold out" by accepting stereotypical roles, and Bradley Yamashita, the aspiring young actor full of radical rage and demands that Asians be allowed realistic stage presences.

Again, because both plays are clearly popular with Anglo-American audiences, one is inspired to wonder whether the acceptance of these plays signals, finally, an end to the marginalization of Chineseness or Asianness. Unfortunately, even a superficial examination of the social text reveals that this is not the case. A close interrogation of the scripts reveals an interesting system of literary subversions with significant impact for the social.

Both Gotanda's *Yankee Dawg You Die* and Hwang's *M. Butterfly* set out to dispel stereotypical representations of Asianness. While Gotanda makes the aim explicit in his text, Hwang has said that he set out to do a "deconstructivist *Madame Butterfly*."[5] Toward this end Hwang employed a strategy described in an interview/essay appropriately entitled "Smashing Stereotypes": "I am interested in cutting through . . . all the crap about the way people write about characters from the East. I mean, when these people are written about, it's always in this inscrutable poetic fashion. It's so untrue, and kind of irritating. So my tendency is to go to the other extreme and make it so slangy and contemporary that it is jarring."[6] Hwang's hope, then, is to offer a truer view of Asianness within the space created by the tension between the audience's stereotypical knowledge and his "slangy and jarring" contemporary reality.

Both plays also seem to be scathing indictments of the Western need to demean, stereotype, and psychologically control the Orient and its stage representations. Despite the good intentions, however, these plays are quite traditional in their celebration of theatrical spectacle and tour de force acting. Indeed, their production values are quintessentially of the theatre. Accordingly, traditional or conventional qualities contribute to their broad popularity. As it is clear Asians remain marginalized, one must conclude that either Anglo-American audiences harbor a strong, heretofore-unexploited masochistic tendency or the authors of these pieces have somehow managed to neutralize or deflect their explicit attack on Anglo-American sensibilities. Given the limits of enlightened liberal self-guilt, one must conclude the reasons for the popularity of the plays will be found in the second alternative.

If Hwang sought to locate a new potential vision for Asianness suspended in tension between the stereotypical and his jarringly contemporary reality, then the characters he deploys to do so are of crucial importance. Unfortunately, they often seem to subvert his stated intention. For example, the specifically Asian technical aspects of Hwang's *M. Butterfly*, the kurogo, serve not as characters but rather exist as mere voiceless presences who silently move stage properties about the acting area. Matters get worse as Asian characters are given voice. Comrade Chan (and the other characters played by the same actor) is perhaps even more stereotypical and cartoonish than the worst of the nineteenth-century stereotypes. Chan serves as a sort of caricature of the stereotype whose "jarring" language alienates.

With the traditional stereotype thus disfigured and in place, the character of Song Liling is of paramount significance, because it is out of the tension between this role and the stereotype that a new, hoped-for vision of Chineseness or Asianness will emerge. And it is here that Hwang's project disintegrates, for he offers at best another disfigured stereotype. Because racial and sexual confusion are collapsed into one character, Song Liling exists as a vehicle of massive self-doubt. S/he claims to be working as a spy for the state but admits that he enjoys the life of a transvestite. While s/he stands in for the role of the victimized Chinese character, the claim is made false when his manipulation of Gallimard is revealed through the role reversal at the end of the play. Accordingly, s/he finally comes across as little more than a disfigured transvestite version of the infamous Chinese "dragon lady" prostitute stereotype.[7] After proudly revealing his manhood to Gallimard, s/he covers up with great embarrassment when his Armani slacks are tossed offstage. This pattern of subversion establishes not an articulation of Asian desire but rather affirms a nefarious complicity with Anglo-American desire in its constitution of otherness, both sexual and racial. Moreover, with the displacement of the action into the neutralized alien space of France, the author deflects any need for consideration of actual race relations in America. Within this confused indeterminate site at the intersection of race and gender, only obvious questions can be apprehended. As audiences leave the theatre, racial/sexual identity is not an issue; rather, most spectators are simply incredulous at how for twenty years Gallimard could have confused Song's rectum for a woman's vagina.

Gotanda also uses what could be called "jarring" contemporary language to demythologize stereotypical portrayals of Asianness which are fixed in the first scene of *Yankee Dawg You Die*. He successfully contrasts the attitudes of the two actors confronting the imperatives of working in an industry which is essentially racist. Vincent Chang is revealed to be a Japanese man pretending to be Chinese to gain employment, but the clear linkage between racial disguise and economic imperative makes such deception acceptable. Indeed, it serves to emphasize the handicaps under which Asian American performers must work. Difficulties for the audience arise when it becomes evident that Vincent is gay and that he is obviously ashamed of it. In light of the recent gains made by America's gay/lesbian liberation movement, this race and gender ambivalence is almost enough to crush the unwitting Chinese/Japanese/closet gay into the space of aporia, subverting the most positive aspects of the play before it. Between the cinematic stereotype and this disfigured Chinese actor, little space exists for a new "real" Asian American. It is suggested that Bradley, too, will succumb to Chang's fate. Indeed, before the end of the play the once-radical Bradley has already accepted stereotypical roles, had a nose job, and been warned that within thirty-five years he may be just like "Chinese" actor Vincent Chang (60).

Clearly, the stage characters which both Hwang and Gotanda deploy to replace the earlier stereotypical portrayals are most problematic. In tension with traditional portrayals, their positions create the site for a new Asian stage presence. Unfortunately, at this site for the emergent new image of Asianness, the figures self-destruct at the very moment of their representation, leaving behind only newly disfigured traces. By interrogating David Henry Hwang's *M. Butterfly* and Philip Kan Gotanda's *Yankee Dawg You Die*, one can see the genesis of a new representational strategy, one in which the words offer a clear indictment of the cultural hegemony of the West, while the characters empowered to represent and speak on behalf of the Chinese or Asianness are laughable and grossly disfigured. Thus marginalized, desexed, and made faceless, these Asian characters constitute no threat to Anglo-American sensibilities. Instead, these figures provide a good evening's entertainment and then float as exotic Orientalist fetishes articulating Anglo-American desire now doubly displaced into the new order of stereotypical representations created by Asian Americans.

Most troubling is the possibility that this rupture at the site of representation could be strategic, intentional, a complicitous commodification, a way of exploiting a jarringly contemporary Orient in a manner quite common in the fashion industry. In a public forum such as the theatre, writers must ultimately seek validation in the marketplace. The market being appealed to is clearly Anglo-American.

The popular acceptance of *these* disfigured Chinese characters, despite their Asian American authorship, does not signify an assimilation of the Chinese or Asianness into the American mainstream but rather a mere repositioning of their marginality, and the creation of new "play" figures for the West. It would appear that both writers have fallen into the trap of complicity which Martin Luther King had admonished against: it seems that while their mouths say no their eyes say yes.[8]

Although both Hwang and Gotanda seem cognizant of the problem, they have nonetheless created representations which, because they incorporate recognizably racist aspects of earlier stereotypes, fail to discredit the validity of those stereotypes. In both cases the long-standing history of the stereotype emerges as dominant in the face of failed attempts at subversion.

The possibility that such productions are intentionally in complicity not only with the market economy but also with the imperialist gaze is very troubling. David Henry Hwang's *The Sound of a Voice* (1983), a somewhat cinematic yet sensitive treatment of difficult interactions between a man and a woman, would seem an almost perfect vehicle for showing Asians working through a relationship on the same level as late twentieth-century white America. For reasons which are unclear, the author chose to make the play exotic, replete with Orientalist touches, exotic costumes, peculiar actions, meaningful silences, artfully arranged flowers. Hwang's *FOB* (1981), written while the author was still a college student, features a conflict between a thoroughly Americanized "ABC" (American-Born Chinese) and a recently arrived ".FOB." The "ABC" Dale provides the following definition of the "FOB":

> F-O-B. Fresh Off the Boat. F.O.B. What words can you think of that characterize the FOB? Clumsy, ugly, greasy FOB. Loud, stupid, four-eyed FOB. Big feet. Horny. Like Lenny in *Of Mice and Men*. Very Good. A literary reference. High-water pants. Floods, to be exact. Someone you wouldn't want your sister to marry. If you are a sister, someone you wouldn't want to marry. That assumes we're talking about boy FOBs, of course. But girl FOBs aren't really as . . . FOBish. Boy FOBs are the worst, the . . . pits. They are the sworn enemies . . . of all ABC girls. Before an ABC girl will be seen on Friday night with a boy FOB in Westwood, she would rather burn off her face . . . FOBs can be found in great numbers almost anyplace you happen to be, but there are some locations where they cluster in particularly large swarms. Community colleges, Chinese-club discos, Asian Sororities, Asian Fraternities, Oriental churches, shopping malls, and of course, BEE GEE concerts. How can you spot an FOB? Look out! If you can't answer that, you might be one.[9]

An Anglo-American audience witnesses the establishment of a new order of stereotype, authenticated by its Asian American authorship, in which Chinese Americans overtly disfigure their own. The list of characteristics which Dale ascribes to the FOB bear a striking resemblance to the museumlike list of fetishized aspects of difference employed by Anglo-American writers during the nineteenth century to theatrically stereotype the Chinese.[10] There is no denying the existence of such tensions between different generations of Chinese American immigrant populations, and similar tensions exist between parents and children. However, this stage conflict exists within a context at once fascinating and alienating. It could be said that such conflicts in immigrant American life are universal and therefore inherently interesting. And indeed this was the case in nineteenth-century American theatre where, for example, loutish Italian immigrant representations were laughed off the stage by assimilated Italian Americans attending the theatre. There exists, however, a crucial difference. During the nineteenth century, the stage representation of the boorish, newly arrived Italian immigrant served as a socializing agent, at once allowing the recently assimilated immigrant to claim his new Americanness while denying any connection with the awkward stage representation.

In *FOB*, the conflict between the two factions becomes itself the subject, and the stage seems to offer to Anglo-America an amusing, anthropologically authentic view of an internecine Chinese American conflict. Further, the periodic transformations of Steve, the FOB character, into the romantically exotic Gwan Gung warrior mythologize the play. Thus, Western audiences can remain comfortably alienated without feeling compelled to engage any of the real social issues that are raised. This is typical of the anthropological gaze. An Asian American acquaintance once confided that she enjoyed American gangster and cowboy movies because she found it amusing to watch white America killing itself off.

The degree to which Chinese American audiences, and Asian American audiences in general, have been subjugated by the dominant culture's representational strategies can be seen in Asian American film productions such as C. Y. Lee's musical *Flower Drum Song* (1961) and Arthur Dong's *Forbidden City* (1989). While Lee's musical was clearly fashioned to cater to Anglo-American expectations, *Forbidden City* displays the depth to which this complicitous desire permeates the Asian American consciousness. Produced to show an alternative to the stereotyped reading of Asian American life, *Forbidden City* offers an examination of "the nation's outstanding Oriental nightclub" of 1939 in San Francisco. This commodified Forbidden City was established in the exotic tourist enclave of Chinatown to exploit sailors on leave, and featured scantily clad

Asian American women constituted as willing objects of the gaze. Combining recently filmed interviews with archival footage of acts from the Chinatown nightclub, the film sets out to dispel the notion that Chinese could not sing and dance: "I've heard people say, 'Do Chinese dance? They don't have any rhythm. They have got terrible legs. I think they're bow legged.' " The film suggests that those Chinese Americans who performed at the Forbidden City nightclub could indeed dance and sing, but with a few exceptions, they were generally inferior to the real American product. Most disheartening is the overwhelming sense that those interviewed truly wished to be represented in the stereotypical forms into which Anglo-America had cast Asian America. These Asian American voices, then, along with those of many before them, seem to further validate the now almost anthropologically authenticated view of Chinese America and Asian America in general.

Perhaps the most awkward case is the one of B. D. Wong, an award-winning actor for his portrayal of Song Liling in David Henry Hwang's *M. Butterfly*. After their work on the Broadway hit, Wong and Hwang became highly visible critics of Asian stereotyping. They were among some of the most outspoken critics of the casting choices surrounding the New York production of *Miss Saigon* (1989). Joining others in the Asian American community, they argued for the casting of more Asian Americans in *Miss Saigon*. The producers themselves have advertised *Miss Saigon* as an updated adaptation of *Madama Butterfly*, the very piece which Hwang's play attacks as racist. Accordingly, it seems ironic to say the least that the Asian American community should be lobbying for greater complicity in such a racist production. After failing to convince the producer to alter any of the casting choices, Wong moved on to his next project, a film role in the recently released *Mystery Date* (1991) in which he plays a Mr. Loo, a stereotypical, squawking Chinese mobster. Given validation by such outspoken critics, these anthropologically achieved stereotypes appear entrenched.

This self-subverting Asian American tendency to reinscribe the touristic stereotype ultimately exposes the success of a strategy of exhaustion, in which the victims — in spite of their best intentions and their complaints that their representations have been disfigured by Anglo-America — remain victims. Unfortunately, the dominant culture is not inclined to change, while the Asian American agents who are in a position to effect change have already capitulated. Until more overtly aggressive strategies are employed, it seems Chinese America must remain an exotic Orientalist fetish, a willing souvenir for America's dreams of empire.

11

Imperial Pornographies of Virtuosity

Problematizing Asian American Life

I am invisible . . . simply because people refuse to see me. Like the bodiless heads you see sometimes in circus sideshows, it is as though I have been surrounded by mirrors of hard, distorting glass. When they approach me they see only my surroundings, themselves, or figments of their imagination — indeed, everything and anything except me.
— Ralph Ellison

In one version of Theatre Repère's *The Dragons' Trilogy*, a catered Chinese meal with appetizers was served during the act breaks. It stands as an amusing reminder that oftentimes a meal in Chinatown is Anglo-America's only real exposure to the Chinese in America. Still, given the sorry state of stage and screen representations of Asian Americans, a little tour of Chinatown for dinner might not be a bad way of seeing the Chinese. However, Anglo-American audiences are admonished to remember that both the setting and the food are designed strictly for their consumption.

On a much grander scale, Chineseness is offered for consumption in American amusement parks and circuses. Today the Chinese impersonate themselves as they perform a menu of feats displaying bizarre virtuosity. Like the Chinese "Fakir" in *7 Faces of Dr. Lao*, who brings both terror and wonderment to the frontier town of Abalone, so the 1992 season of the Ringling Brothers and Barnum and Bailey Circus promises "The Amazing Mongolians" who appear before spectators "From Beyond the

Borders of Imagination."[1] In Chicago, the "Peking Circus" appears at the New Regal Theatre on the South side, while "The Chinese Acrobats" appear four times daily at the Six Flags Great America amusement park in one of the northern suburbs. The New Regal Theatre is a touring-house venue in a predominantly African American neighborhood with reasonable ticket prices, while Six Flags Great America is a utopian theme park which offers to all who can afford the considerably higher price of admission the postmodern thrills of living in a great America. Clearly, the People's Republic of China has found an export commodity marketable to all ranges of American spectatorship.

In great America the Chinese acrobats display their virtuosity, amidst the theme restaurants, the roller-coaster thrill rides, merry-go-rounds, and panoptic view ferris-wheellike rides. The acrobats tumble and jump through rings of knives and fire, blindfolded in some cases. They ride unicycles, balance heavy urns on heads, spin plates atop slender rods, perform handstands on top of six vertically stacked chairs, contort themselves into weird shapes without upsetting the precariously balanced plates in hand, and ride nine to a bicycle. All this is included in the price of admission to the park. That the acrobats would transport themselves halfway around the world exclusively for the visual amusement of those spectators assembled truly makes America great. Admittedly, many nationalities have participated in such circus displays, but the Chinese — and Asians in general — seem to have achieved almost fetish status. Great America provides an innocuous Orientalist acrobatic display as wholesome family entertainment which claims amusement value while masking late twentieth-century reinscriptions of earlier racist stereotypes. Wearing an assortment of curiously exotic ornamental costumes which in more self-consciously avant-garde productions might be called postmodern, those on stage are marked as "Chinese," lest they be mistaken for some other ethnicity. Accordingly, the virtuoso performances collapse into the exotic construction of the acrobats to emerge as a performance of Asian identity. Within this context, many of the seemingly arbitrary activities begin to yield troubling resonances.

The menu of "Chinese" acrobatic acts performed in great America is in many ways typical of circus and other such displacing variety performances. The desire to display a mastery over man-made objects or nature is likely universal. Juggling fiery objects and balancing heavy urns and plates are variety performance activities not likely unique to Asia. But what are we to make of the Chinese man who jumps through rings of fire and knives? Indeed, he even tumbles while blindfolded through hoops of fire and knives to land in a handstand. Certainly, he displays a high level of accomplishment. In many circus acts, however, lions and tigers are forced to jump through flaming hoops, and the resulting success is applauded as an assertion of the human trainer's ability to impose control over a wild beast. But for whom does the Chinese acrobat jump, and what might be the significance? Obviously, these self-conditioned "Chinese" jump for the spectator. Like the animal forced to perform actions far beyond its natural range, so the Chinese contortionist twists herself into knots, while taking care to not drop her spinning plates. Interestingly, the contortionist is almost always female.

More troubling is the way in which these traditional events of pure mastery are psychologized. Three performers are deployed to spin plates atop long slender rods, a common routine repeated at virtually every display of this sort. But in Great America, they are constructed as three cooks. Wearing Western chefs' hats, two establish characters as buffoons, while the virtuoso plate spinner remains focused on the task at hand. The two clown chefs perform what could best be described as comic "monkey imitation" routines in which one mimics the actions of the other until the leader tricks his cohort into kissing his ass. The antics of the two distracting chefs continue, while the dedicated plate spinner goes about his business. Finally successful in getting all nine plates spinning, his good work is ultimately subverted by his two cronies who steal the moment. The need to displace a simple virtuoso performance into a psychologizing narrative frame employing kitchen-service workers reinscribes the nineteenth-century position of the Chinese in America. Rendered comic as it refigures the "monkey imitation" plate-breaking scene in *Ah Sin*, the moment amusingly rearticulates both the earlier nineteenth-century fear of Asian virtuosity and a desire to subvert its potential social significance.

A virtuoso balancing act begins as four champagne bottles are placed on top of a five-foot-high pedestal. The performer stacks chair after chair on the foundation of the bottles. Finally achieving a height against which no more chairs can be raised, he does a few handstands in which his feet almost touch the ceiling. After looking to the audience for approval, he climbs back down to earth dismantling the chair ladder as he descends. His ability to go higher thwarted by the ceiling, he is proven simply human.

As the acrobats demonstrate their mastery over objects in the face of limitations, the clearly empowered spectators can assert dominance over the performers, who willingly transform themselves into objects. One woman demonstrates her leg strength as she becomes a fulcrum supporting two other acrobats on opposite ends of a heavy beam. Another performer displays her flexibility as she is objectified, transformed into a rope suspended between two acrobats who turn her for yet another performer in a game of jump rope. And, for the finale, the entire company of twelve transform themselves into a rotating wall supported by the legs of the three performers who constitute the base.

About one third of the way into the event, a performer demonstrates his mastery of the unicycle by negotiating a slalom run through a tight course of champagne bottles. In a more improvisatory mode, the same character, still on a unicycle, hurls a lime into the audience and motions for the spectator catching it to throw the lime back. As the lime flies back at him the acrobat catches it on the point of a long needle held in his mouth. This procedure is repeated some ten or eleven times, with increasing distances from the stage until the projectiles are hurtling back at him from some sixty feet away. His ability to catch the lime with a needle in his mouth is truly remarkable, but his mastery of this ability cannot be perfect, for he misses at least twice in each performance. Several return visits reveal that the misses are likely intentional, occurring at roughly the same time in each performance. Aside from the errant throw that sails far out of his reach, it seems the actor simply lowers his head at the last moment to allow the lime to bounce off his forehead — an appropriate gesture of self-effacement to deny complete virtuosity. In utopian America, complete mastery over everyday objects is at once denied and made Oriental, mystified to yield a comfortable empire of the visual for middle-class America.

The issue of virtuosity, a construction imposed by white America, has been central to Chinese representation in America from the outset. But this virtuosity has always been deployed on a field of denial and displacement, the variety stage. The disfigurement of this Asian virtuosity serves to empower American audiences, as mass amusements must reduce all to the same level. The more self-consciously avant-garde spectator, however, seems to prefer virtuosity made bizarre. Performance artist Spalding Gray's *Swimming to Cambodia* (1985) offers a brutal rendering of yet another type of Oriental mastery:

After you've been fucked, sucked, had your tubes cleaned, toes cleaned and nose cleaned and you're ready for more, you can go rest and relax at a live show. At a live show the women do everything with their vaginas except have babies. One starts with ping-pong balls and a soda fountain glass: Chung, chung, chung, she catches the ball in the glass. Then another brings out a Coca-Cola bottle, a king-size Coke, which she shakes for a long time, really shakes it hard. She works on it and works on it for a long time until — I don't know how, but she does it — she opens it. I don't know if she has a bottle opener in there, or teeth, but the Coke sprays all over the audience (because it's warm and she's shaken it). Then she pours the rest of the Coke into her womb, squats and — woosh — refills the bottle like a Coca-Cola bottling machine.

Then comes the banana. First she shoots a few lame shots, just boring shots like those Russian rockets that are going to sputter and pop and land on our cornfields. One, two, three. Then, for the finale, she aims her vagina down the center aisle like a cannon, loads it with a very ripe banana and — FOOP! — fires it. She almost hit me in the eye, almost hit an Australian housewife in the head. The banana hits the back wall and sticks, then slowly slides down to the floor.[2]

Gray continues to describe a live sex show in which the Asian performers demonstrate "all the *Kama sutra* poses," and declares the Thais the "most beautiful race I've ever seen," while labeling them androgynous. Gray's Thai women, while sexually available and consumable, should not be viewed as a sexual threat to America. Spalding Gray and the character René Gallimard appear to see Asians in much the same way.

Set in Bangkok, this brief section of Gray's monologue purports to describe an activity observed during his involvement with the filming of *The Killing Fields* (1984), a refiguration of the noble savage motif featuring Southeast Asians. On the book cover, Elinor Fuchs lauds *Swimming to Cambodia* as "an artistic culmination for Gray as well as an impressive political breakthrough," while Mike Steele of the *Minneapolis Star and Tribune* calls Gray "a new wave Mark Twain."[3] The allusion to Mark Twain seems apt in the light of Twain's performance with Asian representations. Gray's claim of mere description, despite the material circumstances that might make its articulation marketable, serves to reinscribe for yet another range of spectatorship a stereotype of constructed Asian virtuosity disfigured. This ploy of "subtle" description, with its claim to authenticity, though theatrically marketable, eventually must prove a lie. A deeper understanding of the social text reveals that it was an earlier Anglo touristic expectation of the sexual availability of Asian women that contributed to the creation of the sex tourism industry of which the performance described is a part. Gray, then, merely etches the stereotype more deeply into the American consciousness, even as he offers refigured titillation to the liberal avant-garde spectatorship.

Obviously, both this Asian woman reduced to banana-firing cannon and the lime-catching Chinese acrobat display virtuosity beyond reason, a virtuosity displaced into aporia. As body parts transcend "normal" use, amusing, but ultimately empty, simulations emerge with arbitrarily achieved fetish value. In addition, Gray's objectification of the Asian woman places her in a manageable position, while neutralizing her as a sexual threat to Anglo womanhood, this despite the fact that she narrowly misses hitting an Australian housewife with one of her bananas. Under the sign of art, then, Gray rewrites the sexually available Asian woman, even as the plays from *Madame Butterfly* (1900) to *Miss Saigon* and *Chess* (1988) do.

Under the sign of activism, American antipornography feminist Andrea Dworkin attacks the "pornography" of the photographs by Akira Ishigaki: "Asian women in this country where I live are tied from trees and hung from ceilings and hung from doorways as a form of public entertainment."[4] Linda Williams later attacks Dworkin for claiming a causal linkage between these *Penthouse* magazine photographs and the murder of a Chinese girl in Chapel Hill, North Carolina, whose body was found hanging from a tree.[5] What is distressing in this is that both positions continue an imperialist view that reduces the Asian subject to its own detriment, while preserving for the speaker an objective and finally anthropological perspective. For these positions, Asianness exists only in the abstract, like a commodity whose value changes according to the market's intent.

It is often said that the gaze of the tourist affects the host much more than the visitor. Clearly, the visitor's constructed expectations of Asian female sexual virtuosity and availability helped give birth to the sex industry of Bangkok. The othering gaze of Anglo-America has also affected Asian life in America. While it could be said that Gray's touristic view of Thailand deploys a sexually neutralized Asian woman to fire the banana, the more standard Anglo-American reading might determine that the Asian woman has taken a decidedly sexual turn. The patriarchal dominant culture has institutionalized the status of the neutralized Asian male, while the nineteenth-century construction of the sexually available Asian female has recently been transformed into the "super Jap" or "sleazy Asian girl" (SAG). In general, Asian women in America have come to be perceived as possessing special mastery of sexual practices. Indeed, in California this belief has given rise to what could be called the cult of the SAGophile, Anglo men whose pursuit of SAGs can be read on the personal ad pages of the *San Francisco Bay Guardian*.[6]

The pervasiveness of this construction, while hinted at in films such as *The World of Suzy Wong* (1960) and *Flower Drum Song* (1961) and many others, becomes explicit through pornographic film titles such as the following, cited in the report of the Attorney General's Commission on Pornography: *Asian Anal Girls*, *Asian Ass*, *Asian Slut*, *Asian Suck Mistress*, *Banzai Ass*, *China deSade*, *Oriental Encounters*, *Oriental Sexpress*, *Oriental*

Lust, Oriental Callgirls, Oriental Sexpot, Oriental Squeeze, Oriental Taboo, and *Oriental Techniques of Pain and Pleasure.*[7]

The constructed, sexually available Asian female emerges as commodity of desire — and, indeed, as a sign whose mere presence promises added value to pornographic products. The same survey quotation techniques deployed to sell Spalding Gray's *Swimming to Cambodia* have been used to sell pornography. The box cover for *China deSade* (1987), a video which markets itself as "an Oriental Classic," introduces the star as "the embodiment of the Oriental ideal of perfect sensuality — dedication to forbidden pleasures, obedience to her sexual masters." Porn star Jade East "is one hot little fortune Cookie" in *China Girl* (1989), a video which promises "an exotic world that worships the pursuit of bodily pleasure in ways the Western world hasn't yet begun to imagine. Meet your beautiful hostess, Jade. She's forgotten more about enjoying sex than most people will ever know. Her body is as perfect as ivory, but more yielding and sensual than any flesh you've ever touched. Just sit back, relax, and let the magic of her desparate [*sic*] need to please you take over. East is about to meet West; Jade East, that is and sex will never be the same." Similarly, the box cover for *Girls of the Orient* (1990) offers "wanton women from across the sea [who] possess the power to drive their partners wild with desire, as their oriental orifices take on all cummers! These petite powerhouses do anything to bring their partners to a breathtaking climax, making it a foreign affair they'll never forget." And, from Rikki Lee, who stars in *Jewel of the Orient* (1991), spectators can "learn the secret of the Orient as our Asian goddess guides you through an erotic parade of tantalizing pleasures. Experience the joy that these masters of passion are anxiously willing to share." Or so the producers of these videos would have spectators believe.

The relationship between the promise and the product within seems tenuous at best. It is not clear that these Asian American women who are deployed in the service of video sex interact with the men in ways different from their Anglo counterparts. Still, the presence of the Asian female is deemed sufficient to afford these products some sense of uniqueness. Asianness, with its mysterious virtuousness, proves to be so persuasive and commodified a marker that it is often employed to falsely advertise pornographic products. *Insatiable* (1992) dares the spectator to "catch a wet glimpse at these Oriental bimbos who have nothin' better to do than show ya what they've gott [*sic*]. Let a moistening array of exotic bimbettes torment your aroused glands as they bombard your screen with some of the most explicit sexual fever ever seen!!! Oriental nookies as performed by Daring Oriental Babes!!!" While clearly not intended for the literary elite, *Insatiable*, it should be noted, will disappoint the SAGophile who buys or rents this video because the only Asians present are on the cardboard cover. Ultimately, the absence of Asian bodies in this video has little effect, for the pornography is not a consideration of bodies but rather an exercise in the deployment of fetishized parts. Besides, the mere mention of Asian femaleness is likely sufficient to allow the spectator to undertake the mental completion of the necessary imaginary Asian body. So, like the lime bouncing off the acrobat's forehead, this culturally constructed Asianness registers as just another moment on the American variety stage which from the outset has served up Asianness for the dominant culture's consumption — another necessary subversion of the constructed notion of virtuosity that surrounds the Asian in America.

To this day, the Anglo desire to disfigure a representation of the sublimated fear of Asian performance can be seen across all ranges of spectatorship. Indeed, the unreasoning fear of the overachieving Asian and of the expatriation of precious Anglo-American capital are little more than refigurations of the nineteenth-century constructions already discussed. In today's text, the construction of the myth of the Asian "model minority" serves as a mechanism for limiting upward mobility. Likewise, the reconstitution of the anti-Asian balance-of-payment problem in international trade merely refigures the fear of an overachieving Asia. In both representational and material terms, these images, which at times drive America to distraction, are problems of the Anglo-American's own making, awkward adjustments to the containment and control mechanisms created to deal with that debased, filthy race which was so inferior to Anglo-America, yet so capable of threatening American labor.

Within this context the possibility of successful mass marketing of Asian representations that are not disfigured is grim to say the least.

David Henry Hwang, Philip Gotanda, and Arthur Dong, to name but a few, have strenuously contested stereotypes. Unfortunately, their overt, powerful attacks have been for nought, because they have chosen to attack the stereotype while reinscribing it in newly disfigured characters to gain popular acceptance among Anglo-American audiences. The failure of such self-subverting attacks on the stereotype can be seen in the fact that even before Hwang's *M. Butterfly* had completed its run, *Miss Saigon*, a new variant on the *Madama Butterfly* theme, opened in London, with Americans clamoring to patronize the subsequent New York production. This inability to dislodge stereotypes suggests the need for a reassessment of the very possibility of creating any noncomplicitous representations of Asianness which can succeed with Anglo-American audiences, for clearly, only representations which reinscribe the stereotype in some form can find success on the popular stage.

Few playwrights have tried to circumvent this imperative to reinscribe the stereotype while attacking the representational apparatus of Anglo-America. In the 1970s, Frank Chin provided some of Asian America's earliest overt attacks on Anglo-American representational practice. Both his *The Chickencoop Chinaman* (1972) and *The Year of the Dragon* (1974) largely avoided the reinscription of the stereotype by providing Asian characters with significant, if eccentric, substance, while often relegating Anglo characters to stereotype. Particularly amusing is the white son-in-law character, Ross, in *The Year of the Dragon*, who, as a "sincerely interested student of all things Chinese," fancies himself "more Chinese" than his Chinese American wife.[8] Further, Chin's portrayal of domestic tensions in Chinatown in *The Year of the Dragon* serves finally to disfigure the colorful touristic perception of a community which in reality often exists as a dead-end economic ghetto for many of its inhabitants. Such uncompromising portrayals did not meet with success on the popular American stage. Chin's lack of success in the face of *M. Butterfly*'s subsequent popularity clearly confirms the need for the reinscription of stereotype as a formula for acceptance by Anglo-American audiences.

Indeed, as film and television have taken the lead in the creation of representational desire, it becomes clear that realistic portrayals of do-

Miss Saigon. *Joan Marcus.*

mestic Asian American life will continue to have difficulty finding an audience, while projects featuring Asians involved in violence and death will command the popular consciousness. Accordingly, such worthy films as the following will be relegated to positions of very limited release due to low audience interest: *Lonely in America* (1990) and *Sam and Me* (1991), two sensitive films dealing with Asian Indian adjustments to life in America and Canada; *An Unremarkable Life* (1989), a quiet film depicting problems with interracial love in retirement years; *The Wash* (1988), a film from an earlier play by Gotanda, which examines the disintegration of an Asian American family; *Eat a Bowl of Tea* (1989), which offers a glimpse of Chinese American domestic life in the years following World War II; *Dim Sum* (1985), which places filial piety in tension with a Chinese daughter's self-actualization; and *Chan is Missing* (1982), a breakthrough independent production which spoofs traditional Hollywood film noir practice, while providing a look at Chinese attitudes as they impact on a search for a missing person. In contrast, films featuring stereotypes and violence, such as *Year of the Dragon* (1985, not to be confused with Frank Chin's 1974 play of the same title), *China Girl* (1987), and *Casualties of War* (1989), will command the popular consciousness. Box-office appeal shows clearly the extent to which popular stereotypes shape audience expectations.

Perhaps this racially limited market should be viewed in a positive light. It is clear that representations offering realistic treatments of everyday life in Asian America will likely fail to achieve broader distribution, because Anglo-America patronizes products that affirm the position of the dominant culture. Still, honest films detailing Asian life in America continue to come out every year, and as the Asian population continues to grow, a discrete and profitable market for these films will emerge.

The theatre production of Asian America has thus far appealed to the mass audience, with venues conveniently situated for dominant-culture marketing. Often little more than compradore enterprises, many Asian theatre companies have served as showcases for Asian talent in search of roles in larger Anglo productions. In 1926, after decrying the "not yet thoroughly normal" portrayals of African Americans, W. E. B. Du Bois laid down the fundamental principles for a new theatre movement:

> The plays of a real Negro theatre must be: 1. *About us*. That is they must have plots which reveal Negro life as it is. 2. *By us*. That is they must be written by Negro authors who understand from birth and continual association just what it means to be a Negro today. 3. *For us*. That is, the theatre must cater primarily to Negro audiences and be supported and sustained by their entertainment and approval. 4. *Near us*. The theatre must be in a Negro neighborhood near the mass of ordinary Negro people.[9]

The implications for Asian America — and indeed for any marginalized group seeking to gain control of its representations — are clear. Asian America must use the representational apparatus to produce material that can convince its own "masses" that they are worthy of more than a mere moment in a freak show, the displacing panoptic of the white American dream. For only then will the representational projects of Asian America begin the difficult task of dismantling Asian American invisibility for the Anglo community as well.

Notes

1. Introduction: Siting Race/Staging Chineseness

1. Aristotle, *The Politics*, I, ii, pp. 59--60; and of course the text goes on to discuss the utility of slavery.

2. Genesis 2:8.

3. Rudolf Wittkower, "Marvels of the East: A Study in the History of Monsters," *Journal of the Warburg and Courtauld Institute* 5 (1942), p. 195. Many reproductions of the early graphic representations of these monstrous Eastern races are included in this fine essay.

4. Mary B. Campbell, *The Witness and the Other World: Exotic European Travel Writing, 400–1600*, pp. 154–161.

5. Leonardo Olschki, "Asiatic Exoticism in Italian Art of the Early Renaissance," *Art Bulletin* 26 (March 1944), p. 105. See also Iris Origo, "The Domestic Enemy: The Eastern Slaves in Tuscany in the Fourteenth and Fifteenth Centuries," *Speculum: A Journal of Mediaeval Studies* 30 (July 1955), pp. 321–366. This situation provides some insight into why late sixteenth-century British drama fixated on the Italian as a platform for the discussion of issues which could not be directly addressed relative to Elizabeth I's reign.

6. Paolo Giovio, *Elogia Virorum bellica virtute illustrium* (Basle, 1575), speaking of Ippolito de' Medici, as quoted in Jacob Burkhardt, *The Civilization of the Renaissance in Italy*, pp. 151–152.

7. See, for example, Eugene Franklin Wong, *On Visual Media Racism: Asians in American Motion Pictures*; Russell Leong, ed., *Moving the Image: Independent Asian Pacific American Media Arts*; and Renée E. Tajima, "Lotus Blossoms Don't Bleed: Images of Asian Women," in *Making Waves: An Anthology of Writings By and About Asian American Women*, ed. Diane Yen-Mei Wong, pp. 308–317.

8. Laura Mulvey, "Visual Pleasure and Narrative Cinema," *Art After Modernism: Rethinking Representation*, ed. Brian Wallis, p. 362, originally published in *Screen* 16 (Autumn 1975), pp. 5–18.

2. The Panoptic Empire of the Gaze: Authenticity and the Touristic Siting of Chinese America

1. *New York Mercury*, 1 January 1781, quoted in Isaac Newton Phelps-Stokes, *Iconography of Manhattan Island* 5:1125.

2. George C. D. Odell, *Annals of the New York Stage* 1:279.

3. [New York] *Daily Advertiser*, 20 January 1790, quoted in Odell, *Annals* 1:285.

4. [New York] *Minerva*, 13 July 1796.

5. Odell, *Annals* 2:306.

6. Unsigned review of *A Chinese Honeymoon*, *The Theatre* 2 (July 1902), p. 4.

7. Steven Mullaney, "Strange Things, Gross Terms, Curious Customs: The Rehearsal of Cultures in the Late Renaissance," *Representations* 3 (1983), pp. 40–67.

8. Odell, *Annals* 4:42.

9. Ibid., p. 43.

10. Ibid., pp. 105–106.

11. Loren W. Fessler, ed., *Chinese in America: Stereotyped Past, Changing Present*, p. 6.

12. Robert Bogdan, *Freak Show: Presenting Human Oddities for Amusement and Profit*, p. 202.

13. Courier for a performance at Hartford, Connecticut, 6 June 1884, in the collection of the Circus World Museum (Baraboo, Wisconsin).

14. Newspaper clipping, dated 26 October 1884, New Orleans, in the collection of the Circus World Museum (Baraboo, Wisconsin).

15. James J. McCloskey, *Across the Continent; Or Scenes From New York Life, and the Pacific Railroad*, in *America's Lost Plays*, vol. 4, ed. Barret H. Clark, p. 107.

16. Delancey Ferguson, "Mark Twain's Lost Curtain Speeches," *South Atlantic Quarterly* 42 (July 1943), p. 269. Also quoted in Margaret Duckett, *Mark Twain and Bret Harte*, p. 153.

17. Rey Chow, *Women and Chinese Modernity: The Politics of Reading Between West and East*, p. 11. Chow also cites Laura Mulvey's important essay "Visual Pleasure and Narrative Cinema," and Kaja Silverman, *The Subject of Semiotics* (New York: Oxford University Press, 1983), p. 225.

18. See Natalie Rewa, "Clichés of Ethnicity Subverted: Robert Lepage's *La Trilogie des Dragons*," *Theatre History in Canada* 11 (Fall 1990), pp. 148–161, and my review of the same piece in *Theatre Journal* 42 (December 1990), pp. 499–501.

3. Bret Harte and Mark Twain's *Ah Sin*: Locating China in the Geography of the American West

1. For a summary treatment of Twain and Harte's careers, see Margaret Duckett, *Mark Twain and Bret Harte*.

2. Ibid., pp. 143–158.

3. *New York Times*, 1 August 1877, p. 5.

4. Bret Harte and Mark Twain, *Ah Sin*, ed. Frederick Anderson, pp. 10–11. The manuscript of *Ah Sin* is in the Clifton Waller Barrett Library of American Literature at the University of Virginia.

5. In volume 2 of *Roughing It*, Mark Twain elaborates: "They do not need to be taught a thing twice, as a general thing. They are imitative. If a Chinaman were to see his master break up a center table, in a passion, and kindle a fire with it, that Chinaman would be likely to resort to the furniture for fuel forever afterward" (130).

6. The situation which Ah Sin finds himself in is remarkably similar to an encounter experienced by Bret Harte when he visited a Chinese theatre in San

Francisco: "It was noticeable, however, that my unrestrained laughter had a discordant effect, and that triangular eyes sometimes turned ominously toward the 'Fanqui devil'; but as I retired discreetly before the play was finished, there were no serious results." Bret Harte, "John Chinaman," in *Writings of Bret Harte* 14:221.

7. Ferguson, "Mark Twain's Lost Curtain Speeches," *South Atlantic Quarterly* 42 (July 1943), p. 269. Also quoted in Margaret Duckett, *Mark Twain and Bret Harte*, p. 153.

8. *The World: New York*, 1 August 1877, p. 5.

9. *People v. Hall*, 4 Cal. 399 (1854).

10. For a summary treatment of this increasingly anti-Chinese legislation, see Elmer Clarence Sandmeyer, *The Anti-Chinese Movement in California.*

11. Harte, "John Chinaman," in *Writings of Bret Harte* 14:220.

12. Harte, "Wan Lee, The Pagan," in *Writings of Bret Harte* 2:264.

13. Harte, "See Yup," in *Writings of Bret Harte* 16:144.

14. Harte, "John Chinaman," in *Writings of Bret Harte* 14:221.

15. *New York Times*, 1 August 1877, p. 5, and *The World: New York*, 1 August 1877, p. 5.

16. Jean Baudrillard, *In the Shadow of the Silent Majorities*, pp. 9–10.

17. The poker illustrations come from a volume of republished pieces. Harte, "Plain Language From Truthful James," in *Writings of Bret Harte* 12:129–131. The illustrations provide an interesting visual intertext to nineteenth-century perceptions of the Chinese. Inspired by a piece entitled "That Heathen Chinee," the wily Ah Sin character first appeared in 1870 in the *Overland Monthly*. In "That Heathen Chinee," Ah Sin wins at poker by cheating. It is curious that seven years later Mark Twain and Bret Harte would remove this assertive activity from the play. Clearly, the Chinese presence on the American frontier was beginning to develop into an economic threat.

18. Duckett, *Mark Twain and Bret Harte*, pp. 119–158.

19. *The World: New York*, 1 August 1877, p. 5.

20. Mark Twain, "John Chinaman in New York," in *Sketches*, p. 278.

21. For the self-perpetuating production of Orientalist fetishes, see Edward W. Said, *Orientalism*; Edward W. Said, "Orientalism Reconsidered," in *Literature, Politics & Theory: Papers from the Essex Conference 1976–84*, eds. Francis Barker, Peter Hulme, Margaret Iversen, and Diana Loxley, pp. 210–229; and Warren I. Cohen, ed., *Reflections on Orientalism: Edward Said, Roger Bresnahan, Surjit Dulai, Edward Graham, and Donald Lammers.*

4. Henry Grimm's *The Chinese Must Go*: Theatricalizing Absence Desired

1. *An Address to the People of the United States Upon the Evils of Chinese Immigration*, prepared by a Committee of the Senate of the State of California, pp. 30–31.

2. Ibid., p. 31.

3. Ibid., pp. 43, 46.

4. Ibid., pp. 25–26.

5. M. B. Starr, *The Coming Struggle; or What the People on the Pacific Coast Think of the Coolie Invasion*, p. 22.

6. *An Address to the People of the United States Upon the Evils of Chinese Immigration*, p. 46.

7. Ibid., p. 20.

8. *Ah Sin*, p. 53.

9. *An Address to the People of the United States Upon the Evils of Chinese Immigration*, p. 43.

10. David D. Utter, "The Chinese Must Go," *The Unitarian Review and Religious Magazine* 12 (July 1879), p. 56.

11. (Shih-shan) Henry Tsai, *The Chinese Experience in America*, pp. 41–42 and Utter, pp. 53–54.

12. *An Address to the People of the United States Upon the Evils of Chinese Immigration*, p. 20.

13. Ibid., p. 45.

14. Henry Grimm, *The Chinese Must Go*, pp. 18–19. This title seems to be available only at the Bancroft Library on the Berkeley campus of the University of California. Located in a bound volume of nineteenth-century anti-Chinese literature, the farce, whose production history is unclear, offers a rare theatrical example of a virulent strain of hate literature.

15. For a detailed treatment of Chinese immigration and the reduction of American labor to machine, see Starr, *The Coming Struggle*, pp. 86–87.

16. For a treatment of the Six Companies, see James A. Whitney, *The Chinese and the Chinese Question*, pp. 116–124; for Chinese slavery, see L. T. Townsend, *The Chinese Problem*, pp. 50–51; and for Chinese as subjects of imperial will, see Robert Wolter, *A Short and Truthful History of the Taking of California and Oregon by the Chinese in the Year* A.D. *1899*, pp. 40–41.

17. Disguises, in fact, surface everywhere in Grimm's play, not only in the possibility of Asian racial-sexual deception but also in the China girls' passing as men to avoid deportation, in Slim Chunk Pin's assuming a white's power when he threatens the Blaine family, and in Frank Blaine's masquerading as his sister to steal from her lover. Indeed, as the farce closes, Frank Blaine, in a plot to steal money, pretends to be the Chinese woman Sam Gin expects from China. Within this sequence can be found all manner of gendered deception and evil. Frank Blaine's use of disguise to rob his sister's lover reminds the viewer that such practices can be useful only in illegal enterprises.

5. Panoptic Containment: The Performance of Anthropology at the Columbian Exposition

1. Many texts from the era dealt with the use of Christian doctrine to justify America's treatment of the native peoples. See, for example, Wilcomb E. Washburn, ed., *The Indian and the White Man*.

2. Ronald T. Takaki, *Iron Cages: Race and Culture in 19th Century America*, p. 231.

3. Takaki, p. 237. See also Tsai, *The Chinese Experience in America*, pp. 22–23, 98.

4. Harte, "Further Language From Truthful James," in *Writings of Bret Harte* 12:165–167. Writings dealing with this growing Sinophobia throughout the late nineteenth century include Starr, *The Coming Struggle*; Townsend, *The Chinese Problem*; Whitney, *The Chinese and the Chinese Question*; and Bret Harte in numerous pieces for the *Overland Monthly*.

5. Tsai, *The Chinese Experience in America*, p. 78. For a detailed treatment of the Wyoming event, see Isaac Hill Bromley, *The Chinese Massacre at Rock Springs, Wyoming Territory, September 2, 1885*.

6. Sucheng Chan, *Asian Americans: An Interpretive History*, p. 54.

7. Tsai, *The Chinese Experience in America*, p. 98.

8. Halsey C. Ives, *The Dream City: A Portfolio of Photographic Views of the World's Columbian Exposition*, p. 2. It should be noted that save for the first two pages, this is an unpaginated portfolio of photographs with descriptive captions on each sheet. Captioned views of both the "Quackuhl" and the Penobscot Indians appeared in this volume.

9. *Portfolio of Photographs of the World's Fair*, unpaginated, photograph with caption.

10. Many photographic volumes dealing with the "racial types" of the Midway survive. See, for example, F. W. Putnam, *Oriental and Occidental Northern and Southern Portrait Types of the Midway Plaisance*. His portfolios promised to display all the "distinctive traits and peculiarities" of the racial groups shown. Putnam was a professor of ethnology at Harvard University.

11. *Illustrated World's Fair: Official Roster of The World's Columbian Exposition* (February 1893), p. 449.

12. Ibid., p. 449.

13. China's first "official" participation would take place in 1904 at the St. Louis World's Fair. See Irene E. Cortinovis, "China at the St. Louis World's Fair," *Missouri Historical Review* 72 (October, 1977), pp. 59–66.

14. *Illustrated World's Fair: Official Roster of The World's Columbian Exposition* (April 1893), p. xvi.

15. Ives, *The Dream City*, unpaginated photograph titled "Chinese Joss-House."

16. Ibid., unpaginated photograph titled "The Chinese Theatre."

17. This cross-dressed disguise seems an early attempt to institutionalize the issues which Grimm used in *The Chinese Must Go* and which Hwang would later raise in *M. Butterfly*. For a detailed treatment of this phenomenon, see Marjorie Garber, *Vested Interests: Cross-Dressing & Cultural Anxiety*.

18. Ives, *The Dream City*, two unpaginated photographs on same page titled "Chinese Beauty" and "Chinese Female Impersonator."

6. Animating the Chinese: Psychologizing the Details

1. One of the most amusing proposals for the containment of the Chinese involved relocating all of San Francisco's Asian population to Yerba Buena, an

island between San Francisco and Oakland. Robert Wolter, the originator of the plan, mused over how the island would appear from the land: "Chinese Junks with their peculiar sails. . . . night comes on, and a fairy scene succeeds — a terraced island decorated with numberless lanterns of various hues. 'A strange and pleasing scene — surely an enchanted island in the Yellow Sea!' " Wolter, *A Short and Truthful History of the Taking of California and Oregon by the Chinese*, pp. 25–27.

2. This text by Will Irwin appears in Arnold Genthe, *Pictures of Old Chinatown*, p. 12.

3. Frederick E. Shearer, ed., *The Pacific Tourist*, p. 279. It should be noted that this travel guide also advertises itself as a complete "Illustrated Trans-Continental Guide of Travel from the Atlantic to the Pacific Ocean." It records much of the panoptic way of observing displayed earlier in McCloskey's *Across the Continent; Or Scenes From New York Life and the Pacific Railroad* (1870). Indeed, the consistency of this touristic perception of Chineseness extends as far back as 1584, if not earlier. See letter of Matteo Ricci, 13 September 1584, as quoted in Jonathan D. Spence, *The Memory Palace of Matteo Ricci*, p. 43.

4. This text by John Kuo Wei Tchen appears in Arnold Genthe, *Genthe's Photographs of San Francisco's Old Chinatown*, p. 15.

5. Arnold Genthe, *As I Remember*, p. 32.

6. See Edward Curtis, *The North American Indian*; Christopher M. Lyman, *The Vanishing Race and Other Illusions: Photographs of Indians by Edward S. Curtis*.

7. Genthe and Irwin, opposite p. 38.

8. Genthe and Tchen, p. 13.

9. Ibid., p. 76.

10. Genthe and Irwin, opposite p. 10.

11. Genthe and Tchen, p. 75.

12. Genthe and Irwin, pp. 4–5.

13. Ibid., p. 24.

14. Ibid., pp. 30–31.

15. Ibid., p. 33.

16. Ibid., opposite p. 26.

17. Ibid., recto page preceding p. 19.

18. Ira M. Condit, *The Chinaman As We See Him*, p. 170.

19. Genthe and Irwin, p. 3.

20. Genthe, *As I Remember*, p. 38.

21. Raymond Fielding, *The American Newsreel 1911–1967*, pp. 40–43.

7. *Casualties of War*: The Death of Asia on the American Field of Representation

1. Catherine Clement, *Opera, Or the Undoing of Women*, p. 8.

2. Obituary newsclip, dated 4 February 1961, from the "Anna May Wong" file, Wisconsin Center for Film and Theatre Research, Wisconsin State Historical Society (Madison, Wisconsin). Boldface copy above the AP dateline

reads: "Anna M. Wong Film Siren of Mystery Dies. Career Story: She Died A Thousand Deaths."

3. "Anna May Wong Dies at 54," *New York Herald Tribune*, 5 February 1961, from the "Anna May Wong" file, Wisconsin Center for Film and Theatre Research.

4. An obvious omission is the constructed comically self-subverting China-man resulting from an interracial relationship. The title character of the 1895 play *Patsy O'Wang* by T. S. Denison comes to mind. Born of an Irish father and a Chinese mother, Patsy O'Wang develops a comic, but ultimately disfiguring, peculiarity: whiskey, "the drink of his father transforms him into a true [wild] Irishman, while strong tea, the beverage of his mother, has the power of restoring fully his Chinese character." This comic potential is exploited throughout the play and would later be incorporated into many projects which appear to offer positive portrayals of Asians interacting with Anglo-America.

8. Eugene O'Neill's *Marco Millions*: Desiring Marginality and the Dematerialization of Asia

1. Arthur Gelb and Barbara Gelb, *O'Neill*, p. 563. For detailed treatments of the evolution of this play, see John H. Stroupe, "*Marco Millions* and O'Neill's 'Two Part Two-Play' Form," *Modern Drama* 13 (February 1971), pp. 382–392; Virginia Floyd, ed., *Eugene O'Neill at Work*, pp. 57–67. The uncut longer version of *Marco Millions* is available in Travis Bogard, ed., *The Unknown O'Neill*, pp. 195–307.

2. *New York Times*, 10 January 1928, p. 28.

3. *New York Daily Mirror*, 11 January 1928, p. 27.

4. *The World* (New York), 10 January 1928, p. 28.

5. *New York Times*, 10 January 1928, p. 28.

6. An Min Hsia, "The Tao and Eugene O'Neill" (Ph.D. diss., Indiana University, 1979), p. 71. Hsia's dissertation, along with a later piece, "Cycle of Return: O'Neill and the Tao," in *Eugene O'Neill's Critics: Voices From Abroad*, ed. Horst Frenz and Susan Tuck, pp. 169–173, provides interesting treatments of Taoist influences on this O'Neill play. Of note is the Taoist active/passive dichotomy which clearly intrigued O'Neill.

7. Floyd, ed. *Eugene O'Neill at Work*, p. 57. Floyd reports that O'Neill's "large collection of 'millions of notes,' excerpts from *The Travels of Marco Polo*, the historical hero's actual account of his journey to the East and stay at the court of the Great Kaan" has survived and is available at Yale University's Beinecke Library.

8. Marco Polo, *The Book of Ser Marco Polo, The Venetian Concerning the Kingdoms and Marvels of the East* 1:418.

9. Eugene O'Neill, *Marco Millions*, p. 94.

10. *Herald Tribune* (New York), 10 January 1928, p. 28.

11. *New York Times*, 10 January 1928, p. 28.

12. Ironically, in the fall of 1928 O'Neill would pay a visit to Asia, touring

through Ceylon, Saigon, Singapore, Hong Kong, and Shanghai. The Gelbs report that despite "his high hopes, O'Neill ultimately found no peace or satisfaction in the East" (680). Later, the Gelbs quote Mai-mai Sze, a close friend of the O'Neills, saying that "Gene and Carlotta traveled to the East like a pair of tourists" (686). See also Horst Frenz, "Eugene O'Neill and China," *Tamkang Review* 8 (Fall/Winter 1979), pp. 5–16, for an interesting study on this subject.

13. See Said, *Orientalism*; Said, "Orientalism Reconsidered"; Cohen, ed., *Reflections on Orientalism*.

14. Indeed, this sense of the panoptic vision is even more pronounced in the earlier uncut version of *Marco Millions* because cinematic displacements serve as bookendlike devices in act 1, scene 2, and act 8, scene 1. See Bogard, ed., *The Unknown O'Neill*, pp. 196, 204–211, 296–301.

9. Disfiguring *The Castle of Fu Manchu*: Racism Reinscribed in the Playground of the Postmodern

1. Tsai Chin, *Daughter of Shanghai*, p. 144.

10. Flawed Self-Representations: Authenticating Chinese American Marginality

1. For detailed treatment, see Donald M. Lowe, *History of Bourgeois Perception*.

2. *M. Butterfly* premiered on 10 February 1988 at the National Theatre in Washington, D.C., and opened in New York City on Broadway on 20 March 1988 at the Eugene O'Neill Theatre. All references to the playscript are from the first publication of the play, which appeared as an insert (with independent internal pagination) between pages 32 and 33 of *American Theatre* (July/August 1988).

3. Philip Kan Gotanda, "Yankee Dawg You Die," typescript provided by the Wisdom Bridge Theatre Company of Chicago, which produced the piece during the fall of 1988.

4. David Savran, *In Their Own Words*, p. 127.

5. David Henry Hwang, *M. Butterfly* (New York: New American Library, 1989), p. 95.

6. Gerard Raymond, "Smashing Stereotypes," *Theatre Week* (11 April 1988), p. 8. See also Savran, pp. 117–131.

7. For a treatment of this stereotype as it developed in the American cinema, see Tajima, "Lotus Blossoms Don't Bleed: Images of Asian Women," in *Making Waves: An Anthology of Writings By and About Asian American Women*, pp. 308–317.

8. It is interesting to note that in responding to "leftist element[s], which might accuse me of selling out," Hwang has said, "I think the [Chinese American] community by and large is very success oriented and is more likely to embrace one of their own on the basis of having got to Broadway, no matter

what the play was — as long as it was not horribly critical of the Chinese-American community." Raymond, p. 8.

9. David Henry Hwang, *FOB*, in *FOB and The House of Sleeping Beauties*, p. 13.

10. See, for example, Arthur H. Smith, *Chinese Characteristics*.

11. Imperial Pornographies of Virtuosity: Problematizing Asian American Life

1. From the centerfold poster stapled into the Ringling Brothers and Barnum and Bailey Circus Program for 1992.

2. Spalding Gray, *Swimming to Cambodia*, pp. 42–43.

3. Quoted on cover and first inside recto page of *Swimming to Cambodia*.

4. Quoted from *Final Report of the Attorney General's Commission on Pornography*, p. 198. The "pornographic" photographs attacked by Dworkin have been defended as artistic projects. See photographs by Akira Ishigaki, "Sakura," *Penthouse* (December 1984), pp. 118–127.

5. See Linda Williams, *Hard Core*, pp. 20–21; Ishigaki, "Sakura"; "Suspect Held in Hanging of an 8-Year Old Girl," *New York Times*, 4 February 1985, sec. 1, p. 8.

6. See Ann Cherian, "Reorientations: Asian-Americans at Berkeley," *California Monthly* 97 (September 1986), pp. 32–33, 38; Joan Walsh, "Asian Women, Caucasian Men: The New Demographics of Love," *San Francisco Examiner*, 2 December 1990, *Image Magazine* section, pp. 11–17.

7. Quoted from an extensive list of pornographic films in *Final Report of the Attorney General's Commission on Pornography*, pp. 388–433.

8. Frank Chin, *The Year of the Dragon*, in *Chickencoop Chinaman/The Year of the Dragon: Two Plays by Frank Chin*, pp. 78–79.

9. W. E. B. Du Bois, "Krigwa Players Little Negro Theatre," *The Crisis* 32 (July 1926), p. 134. Some fifty years later Yen Lu Wong, "Chinese American Theatre," *TDR* 20.2 (1976), pp. 13–18, would make a similar plea with mixed results.

Bibliography

An Address to the People of the United States Upon the Evils of Chinese Immigration. Prepared by a Committee of the Senate of the State of California, 13 August 1877.

Ambler, Louise Todd, and Melissa Banta, eds. *The Invention of Photography and Its Impact on Learning.* Cambridge: Harvard University Library, 1989.

Aristotle. *The Politics.* Translated by T. A. Sinclair. London: Penguin, 1981.

Banta, Melissa, and Curtis M. Hinsley. *From Site to Sight: Anthropology, Photography, and the Power of Imagery.* Cambridge: Peabody Museum Press, 1986.

Baudrillard, Jean. *In the Shadow of the Silent Majorities,* trans. Paul Foss, Paul Patton, and John Johnston. New York: Semiotext(e), 1983.

[Blake, Alexander V.] *Anecdotes of the American Indians, Illustrating their Eccentricities of Character.* Hartford: C. M. Wells, 1850.

Bogard, Travis, ed. *The Unknown O'Neill.* New Haven: Yale University Press, 1988.

Bogdan, Robert. *Freak Show: Presenting Human Oddities for Amusement and Profit.* Chicago: University of Chicago Press, 1988.

Boucher, Philip P. *Cannibal Encounters: European and Island Caribs, 1492–1763.* Baltimore: Johns Hopkins University Press, 1992.

Brenkman, John. *Culture and Domination.* Ithaca: Cornell University Press, 1987.

Bromley, Isaac Hill. *The Chinese Massacre at Rock Springs, Wyoming Territory, September 2, 1885.* Boston: Franklin Press, 1886.

Bruckner, Paul. *The Tears of the White Man: Compassion as Contempt,* trans. William R. Beer. New York: Free Press, 1986.

Burkhardt, Jacob. *The Civilization of the Renaissance in Italy.* Vienna: Phaidon Press, 1937.

Caldwell, Dan. "The Negroization of the Chinese Stereotype in California." *Southern California Quarterly* 53 (March 1971), pp. 123–131.

Campbell, Mary B. *The Witness and the Other World: Exotic European Travel Writing, 400–1600.* Ithaca: Cornell University Press, 1988.

Chan, Sucheng. *Asian Americans: An Intrepretive History.* Boston: Twayne Publishers, 1991.

Cherian, Anne. "Reorientations: Asian-Americans at Berkeley." *California Monthly* 97 (September 1986), pp. 32–33, 38.

Chin, Frank. *Chickencoop Chinaman/The Year of the Dragon: Two Plays by Frank Chin.* Seattle: University of Washington Press, 1988.

Chin, Tsai. *Daughter of Shanghai.* New York: St. Martin's Press, 1989.

Chow, Rey. *Women and Modernity: The Politics of Reading Between West and East.* Minneapolis: University of Minnesota Press, 1991.

Chu, Limin. *Images of China and the Chinese in the Overland Monthly, 1868–1875, 1883–1935.* San Francisco: R & E Associates, 1974.

Clement, Catherine. *Opera, Or the Undoing of Women*. Minneapolis: University of Minnesota Press, 1986.

Cohen, Warren I., ed. *Reflections on Orientalism: Edward Said, Roger Bresnahan, Surjit Dulai, Edward Graham, and Donald Lammers*. East Lansing: Michigan State University, Asian Studies Center, 1983.

Comaroff, John, and Jean Comaroff, eds. *Ethnography and the Historical Imagination*. Boulder, Colorado: Westview Press, 1992.

Condit, Ira M. *The Chinaman as We See Him*. New York: Fleming H. Revell, 1900.

Copland, Ian. *The Burden of Empire: Perspectives on Imperialism and Colonialism*. Melbourne: Oxford University Press, 1990.

Cortinovis, Irene E. "China at the St. Louis World's Fair." *Missouri Historical Review* 72 (October 1977), pp. 59–66.

Curtis, Edward. *The North American Indian*. 20 vols. Privately printed, 1907–1930.

Denison, T. S. *Patsy O'Wang*. Chicago: T. S. Denison, 1895.

Drinnon, Richard. *Facing West: The Metaphysics of Indian- Hating and Empire-Building*. New York: New American Library, 1980.

Du Bois, W. E. B. "Krigwa Players Little Negro Theatre." *The Crisis* 32 (July 1926), pp. 134–136.

Duckett, Margaret. *Mark Twain and Bret Harte*. Norman: University of Oklahoma Press, 1964.

Fenn, William Purviance. *Ah Sin and His Brethren in American Literature*. Peiping: California College in China, 1933.

Fessler, Loren W., ed. *Chinese in America: Stereotyped Past, Changing Present*. New York: Vantage Press, 1983.

Fielding, Raymond. *The American Newsreel 1911–1967*. Norman: University of Oklahoma Press, 1972.

Final Report of the Attorney General's Commission on Pornography. Nashville: Rutledge Hill Press, 1986.

Floyd, Virginia, ed. *Eugene O'Neill at Work*. New York: Frederick Ungar, 1981.

Frenz, Horst. "Eugene O'Neill and China," *Tamkang Review* 8 (Fall/Winter 1979), pp. 5–16.

Frenz, Horst, and Susan Tuck, eds. *Eugene O'Neill's Critics: Voices From Abroad*. Carbondale: Southern Illinois Press, 1984.

Garber, Marjorie. *Vested Interests: Cross-Dressing & Cultural Anxiety*. New York: Routledge, 1992.

Gelb, Arthur, and Barbara Gelb. *O'Neill*. New York: Harper & Row, 1987.

Genthe, Arnold. *As I Remember*. New York: Reynal & Hitchcock, 1936.

———. *Genthe's Photographs of San Francisco's Old Chinatown*. Selection and text by John Kuo Wei Tchen. New York: Dover Publications, 1984.

———. *Pictures of Old Chinatown*. With text by Will Irwin. New York: Moffat, Yard, 1908.

———. "The Children of Chinatown." *Camera Craft* 2 (December 1900), pp. 99–104.

Gotanda, Philip Kan. "Yankee Dawg You Die." Typescript. Wisdom Bridge Theatre Company of Chicago, 1988.

Gray, Spalding. *Swimming to Cambodia*. New York: Theatre Communications Group, 1985.

Greenblatt, Stephen. *Marvelous Possessions: The Wonder of the New World*. Chicago: University of Chicago Press, 1991.

Greenhalgh, Paul. *Ephemeral Vistas: The Expositions Universelles, Great Exhibitions and World's Fairs, 1851–1939*. Manchester: Manchester University Press, 1988.

Grimm, Henry. *"The Chinese Must Go": A Farce in Four Acts*. San Francisco: A. L. Bancroft, 1879.

Harris, Neil. *Cultural Excursions: Marketing Appetites and Cultural Tastes in Modern America*. Chicago: University of Chicago Press, 1990.

Harte, Bret. *Writings of Bret Harte*. Standard Library Edition. Boston: Houghton Mifflin, 1896.

Harte, Bret, and Mark Twain. *Ah Sin*, ed. Frederick Anderson. San Francisco: Book Club of California, 1961.

Horne, Donald. *The Great Museum: The Re-presentation of History*. London: Pluto Press, 1984.

Hsia, An Min. "The Tao and Eugene O'Neill." Ph.D. diss., Indiana University, 1979.

Hwang, David Henry. *FOB and The House of Seven Beauties*. New York: Dramatists Play Service, 1983.

———. *M. Butterfly*. New York: New American Library, 1989; originally published in *American Theatre* (July/August 1988).

Isaacs, Harold R. *Scratches on Our Mind: Images of China and India*. New York: John Day, 1958.

Ishigaki, Akira. "Sakura." *Penthouse* (December 1984), pp. 118–127.

Ives, Halsey C. *The Dream City: A Portfolio of Photographic Views of the World's Columbian Exposition*. St. Louis: N. D. Thompson, 1893.

Jakle, John A. *The Tourist: Travel in Twentieth-Century North America*. Lincoln: University of Nebraska Press, 1985.

Jameson, Frederic. *Postmodernism or, The Cultural Logic of Late Capitalism*. Durham: Duke University Press, 1991.

Jones, Dorothy B. *The Portrayal of China and India on the American Screen, 1896–1955*. Cambridge: M.I.T. Center for International Studies, 1955.

Leong, Russell, ed. *Moving the Image: Independent Asian Pacific American Media Arts*. Los Angeles: UCLA Asian American Studies Center, 1991.

Lewis, Bernard. *Race and Slavery in the Middle East*. New York: Oxford University Press, 1990.

Lowe, Donald M. *History of Bourgeois Perception*. Chicago: University of Chicago Press, 1982.

Lyman, Christopher M. *The Vanishing Race and Other Illusions: Photographs of Indians by Edward S. Curtis*. New York: Pantheon Books, 1982.

MacCannell, Dean. *The Tourist: A New Theory of the Leisure Class*. New York: Schocken Books, 1989.

McCloskey, James J. *Across the Continent; Or Scenes from New York Life, and the Pacific Railroad*. In *America's Lost Plays*, vol. 4, ed. Barret H. Clark. Bloomington: Indiana University Press, 1963.

Mascia-Lees, Frances E., and Patricia Sharpe, eds. *Tatoo, Torture, Mutilation, and Adornment: The Denaturalization of the Body in Culture and Text*. Albany: State University of New York Press, 1992.

Melman, Billie. *Women's Orient: English Women and the Middle East, 1718–1918, Sexuality, Religion and Work*. Ann Arbor: University of Michigan Press, 1992.

Moy, James S. "*The Dragon's Trilogy* and *Who Killed the Dragon Lady?*" *Theatre Journal* 42 (December 1990), pp. 499–501.

———. "Subversion of the Pornographic in Mass Entertainments." *Themes in Drama* 7 (1985), pp. 191-201.

———. "Subverting/Alienating Performance Structures." *Themes in Drama* 9 (1987), pp. 161–176.

Mullaney, Steven. "Strange Things, Gross Terms, Curious Customs: The Rehearsal of Cultures in the Late Renaissance." *Representations* 3 (1983), pp. 40–67.

Mulvey, Laura. "Visual Pleasure and Narrative Cinema." *Screen* 16 (Autumn 1975), pp. 5–18.

Nee, Victor G., and Brett de Bary Nee. *Longtime Californ': A Documentary Study of an American Chinatown*. Boston: Houghton Mifflin, 1974.

Odell, George C. D. *Annals of the New York Stage*. 15 vols. New York: Columbia University Press, 1927–1949.

Olschki, Leonardo. "Asiatic Exoticism in Italian Art of the Early Renaissance." *Art Bulletin* 26 (March 1944), pp. 95–106.

O'Neill, Eugene. *Marco Millions*. London: Jonathan Cape, 1927.

Origo, Iris. "The Domestic Enemy: The Eastern Slaves in Tuscany in the Fourteenth and Fifteenth Centuries." *Speculum: A Journal of Mediaeval Studies* 30 (July 1955), pp. 321–366.

Phelps-Stokes, Isaac Newton. *Iconography of Manhattan Island*. 6 vols. New York: Robert H. Hood, 1928.

Polo, Marco. *The Book of Ser Marco Polo, The Venetian Concerning the Kingdoms and Marvels of the East*. Translated by Henry Yule. 2 vols. New York: Charles Scribner's Sons, 1903.

Portfolio of Photographs of the World's Fair. Chicago: Werner Company, 1893.

Price, Sally. *Primitive Art in Civilized Places*. Chicago: University of Chicago Press, 1989.

Pugh, Simon, ed. *Reading Landscape: Country-City-Capital*. Manchester: Manchester University Press, 1990.

Putnam, F. W. *Oriental and Occidental Northern and Southern Portrait Types of the Midway Plaisance*. St. Louis: N. D. Thompson, 1894.

Raymond, Gerard. "Smashing Stereotypes." *Theatre Week* (11 April 1988), p. 8.

Rewa, Natalie. "Cliches of Ethnicity Subverted: Robert Lepage's *La Trilogie des Dragons*." *Theatre History in Canada* 11 (Fall 1990), pp. 148–161.

Robinson, Maxime. *Europe and the Mystique of Islam*, trans. Roger Veinus. Seattle: University of Washington Press, 1991.

Rousseau, G. S., and Roy Porter, eds. *Exoticism in the Enlightenment*. Manchester: Manchester University Press, 1990.

Ryan, Chris. *Recreational Tourism: A Social Science Perspective*. New York: Routledge, 1991.

Said, Edward W. *Orientalism*. New York: Random House, 1979.

———. "Orientalism Reconsidered." In *Literature, Politics & Theory: Papers from the Essex Conference 1976–84*, eds. Francis Barker, Peter Hulme, Margaret Iverson, and Diana Loxley, pp. 210–229. London: Methuen, 1986.

Sandmeyer, Elmer Clarence. *The Anti-Chinese Movement in California*. Urbana: University of Illinois Press, 1973.

Savran, David. *In Their Own Words*. New York: Theatre Communications Group, 1988.

Shearer, Frederick E., ed. *The Pacific Tourist*. New York: Adams & Bishop, 1884.

Silk, Catherine, and John Silk, eds. *Racism and Anti- Racism in American Popular Culture: Portrayals of African-Americans in Fiction and Film*. Manchester: Manchester University Press, 1990.

Slotkin, Richard. *Regeneration Through Violence: The Mythology of the American Frontier, 1600–1860*. Middletown, Connecticut: Wesleyan University Press, 1973.

Smith, Arthur H. *Chinese Characteristics*. New York: Fleming H. Revell, 1894.

Spence, Jonathan D. *The Memory Palace of Matteo Ricci*. New York: Penguin Books, 1984.

Stannard, David E. *American Holocaust: Columbus and the Conquest of the New World*. New York: Oxford University Press, 1992.

Starr, M. B. *The Coming Struggle; or What the People on the Pacific Coast Think of the Coolie Invasion*. San Francisco: Bacon, 1873.

Stroupe, John H. "*Marco Millions* and O'Neill's 'Two Part Two-Play' Form." *Modern Drama* 13 (February 1971), pp. 382–392.

Tajima, Renee E. "Lotus Blossoms Don't Bleed: Images of Asian Women." In *Making Waves: An Anthology of Writings By and About Asian American Women*, ed. Diane Yen-Mei Wong, pp. 308–317. Boston: Beacon Press, 1989.

Takaki, Ronald T. *Iron Cages: Race and Culture in 19th Century America*. New York: Alfred A. Knopf, 1979.

Torgovnick, Marianna. *Gone Primitive: Savage Intellects, Modern Lives*. Chicago: University of Chicago Press, 1990.

Townsend, L. T. *The Chinese Problem*. Boston: Lee and Shepard, 1876.

Tsai, Shih-shan Henry. *China and the Overseas Chinese in the United States, 1868–1911*. Fayetteville: University of Arkansas Press, 1983.

———. *The Chinese Experience in America*. Bloomington: Indiana University Press, 1986.

Twain, Mark. *Roughing It*. New York: Harper & Brothers, 1899.

———. *Sketches*. New York: Harper & Brothers, 1922.

Urry, John. *The Tourist Gaze: Leisure and Travel in Contemporary Societies*. Newbury Park, California: Sage Publications, 1990.

Utter, David D. "The Chinese Must Go." *The Unitarian Review and Religious Magazine* 12 (July 1879), pp. 48- 56.

Wadler, Joyce. "For the First Time, the Real-Life Models for Broadway's *M.*

Butterfly Tell of Their Very Strange Romance." *People* 30 (8 August 1988), pp. 88–98.

Walsh, Joan. "Asian Women, Caucasian Men: The New Demographics of Love." *San Francisco Examiner*, 2 December 1990, *Image Magazine* section, pp. 11–17.

Washburn, Wilcomb E., ed. *The Indian and the White Man*. New York: Anchor Books, 1964.

Whitney, James A. *The Chinese and the Chinese Question*. New York: Tibbals Book Company, 1888.

Williams, Linda. *Hard Core*. Berkeley: University of California Press, 1989.

Wittkower, Rudolf. "Marvels of the East: A Study in the History of Monsters." *Journal of the Warburg and Courtauld Institute* 5 (1942), pp. 159–197.

Wolter, Robert. *A Short and Truthful History of the Taking of California and Oregon by the Chinese in the Year A.D. 1899*. San Francisco: A. L. Bancroft, 1882.

Wong, Eugene Franklin. *On Visual Media Racism: Asians in American Motion Pictures*. New York: Arno Press, 1978.

Wong, Yen Lu. "Chinese American Theatre." *TDR* 20.2 (1976), pp. 13–18.

Studies in Theatre History and Culture

Marginal Sights: Staging the Chinese in America

By James S. Moy

Melodramatic Formations: American Theatre and

Society, 1820–1870

By Bruce A. McConachie

Modern Hamlets and Their Soliloquies

By Mary Z. Maher

The Performance of Power:

Theatrical Discourse and Politics

Edited by Sue-Ellen Case and Janelle Reinelt

Wandering Stars: Russian Emigré Theatre, 1905–1940

Edited by Laurence Senelick